Φ 270

37⁰⁰/¼"

ESSENTIAL
ivorypress

A CRAZY JOB

LEADING PUBLISHERS
IN CONVERSATION WITH
JUAN CRUZ RUIZ

To Isabel Polanco,
to Toni López,
publishers

FOREWORD

The conversations of Juan Cruz with the key publishers of our time mark the beginning of the Ivorypress Essential collection. The editorial team, with Iñaki Domingo as coordinator, has selected works which we consider to be essential from the disciplines of the visual arts, architecture and contemporary design. Ivorypress has decided to launch the Ivorypress Essential collection with a work which highlights the power of the book, of the written word and of the role of the publisher.

I would like to express my gratitude to Juan Cruz – publisher, writer and prolific journalist – for his generous flexibility, and his ability to listen as well as for his open and unconditional attitude towards building bridges of friendship and communication between those of us who dedicate our professional life to this work. My thanks also for his cooperation with the team at Ivorypress during the process of selecting the content and design for the present publication. Juan Cruz is not only an avid reader, but he also understands the intricacies of the publishing universe down to the very detail. He is able to analyse with masterly expertise the critical dilemmas that a publisher must confront every day in order to survive and to bring forward the publishing projects in which one believes and wishes to support unconditionally. This is why I cannot imagine a better orchestrator for this publisher's manifesto in favour of the book.

In every book we read we can observe common traits belonging to the nonetheless disparate characters of the people behind them.

Juan Cruz profiles the personalities and emotions driving publishing houses large and small, who, with intuition and daring, have helped to advance the careers of their writers, some well known and others still emerging. If I had to summarise the characteristics that motivate publishers to continue with their work despite the difficult – but not insuperable – obstacles that have arisen over the last few years, they would be, without a doubt, the limitless capacity to assume constant intellectual and financial risks, the passion to transmit knowledge, ideas and experience, and the projection of a critical portrait of society. These issues are embodied in the works of the writers that one selects to publish, the optimistic determination to embrace the book, and finally and above all, an unconditional love for the publishing profession. Some of the conversations collected in this book were published in the Spanish daily newpaper *El País* between 2010 and 2011. Others were conducted specially for this book over the last months of 2011, with the aim of offering a vision of the publishing landscape as broad and diverse as possible.

Along with the team at Ivorypress, I would like to express my gratitude to the publishers who agreed to participate in this project, figures whose professional trajectories I admire and hold as a benchmark in my daily work as a publisher. Specifically, George Weidenfeld, with whom I have maintained a constant exchange of ideas for almost 20 years. His wise and generous advice has contributed to the growth and international expansion of Ivorypress. But above all I would like to thank him for the indefatigable manner in which he develops publishing projects, as well as for his cosmopolitan and holistic vision of the figure of the publisher, who should, in his opinion, be constantly searching to achieve the ethical and aesthetic survival of the book. I would also like to express my gratitude to Robert Silvers who is editor of *The New York Review of Books*. I very much appreciate his open gesture of showing me the workspace in which he spends so many hours, and the small bedroom without windows, backing onto a diminutive bathroom, with no more than a bed, an armchair, a lamp and some simple bookshelves overflowing with books in the process of being read. Many are the days when Robert Silvers sleeps in this minute space, literally just a step away from his office and no more than two square metres, when he finishes editing *The New York Review of Books* at five o'clock in the morning and it's no longer worth taking a taxi home. Instead, he sleeps here for three hours or so, and then finds himself ready to receive his team to begin another day's work.

There is no point in paraphrasing what can be read throughout the following pages. The unstoppable growth of the digital world, the specialisation of publishing houses and the segmentation of the market, the importance of non-stop promotion, the perhaps inevitable symbiosis of the figures of literary agent, publisher, librarian and bookseller, are themes which are being analysed from different angles and which converge into an uncertain but at the same time stimulating and hopeful future for the book and the task of the publisher.

I would like this first publication, which marks the beginning of the collection, to become an ever shining beacon for young publishers who are now starting out and who believe in the strength and power of the book.

Elena Ochoa Foster
Founder and CEO of Ivorypress

RICCARDO CAVALLERO

General Manager of Trade Books at Mondadori Group
for Italy, Spain & Latin America

THE POWER IS PASSING FROM THE EDITOR TO THE READER

'The power is passing from the editor to the reader', says Riccardo Cavallero as he proposes strategies for dealing with the new situation in the world of publishing. Gutenberg is still alive and well, and will continue to be, but the Internet, 'the digital world' as he calls it, already points to the future.

Riccardo Cavallero is General Manager of Trade Books at Mondadori Group for Italy, Spain and Latin America. He was born near Turin in 1962. Trained as an economist, he has held a variety of editorial posts, first with Grijalbo and then with Random House Mondadori. His task has been a managerial one, first as chief executive at Random House Mondadori in New York and subsequently in Barcelona.

Are we facing a real change?

Yes, for the first time the world of publishing is really changing. Digital technology is having a major impact, because power is passing from the editor to the reader. Since Gutenberg, nothing had really changed. There were mechanical and technical changes, but the process and the business remained the same. Editors had the power to decide what would or would not be read in a country, though on occasion they misunderstood their role, which they confused with that of the printer or distributor.

And with the digital book, that has changed.

The power passes to the reader, who is the one who decides what he wants, when he wants it, how he wants it and at what price. This is the big change.

And is this change being easily accepted?

The publishing world is not ready for this. What will make all the difference—as with the dinosaurs—is that survival will require a change of habitat. And there are many who at the moment lack the strength of mind to realise that and modify their way of working accordingly.

At least the e-book has already occupied its territory... and the publishing houses are the ones who are adopting it.

The e-book in itself means nothing. It was born old already. The important thing is the digital revolution. We have to change our way of working by taking account of the reader and understanding what they want. Up until now we have been living in a bubble of luxury in which we didn't need to take what the reader wanted into account.

Must the publisher become something different?
There is no doubt he or she will. There was a time when one didn't know whether a publisher was a printer or a distributor... The form of transmission has changed. I believe that in five to ten years the publisher will be a librarian. We will manage content that we will have to lend out. We will no longer be owners of something, but will have in our possession only what we are served at that moment...

So the role of the publisher will be less important?
It will continue to be very important, but it will not be the same, it will be different. The digital revolution is a most remarkable change, but what will not change for a very long while in this development is the mode of creation, of writing. The digital revolution will not influence this in the short term. The writer will experiment. There have already been creations such as SMS books, and even books for mobiles. In this first phase, there's this big bacchanal: the author is convinced the editor is of no further use to him, that it is the agent who has to do his job. There is a huge amount of information available to readers, and they can edit books themselves without any problem, but they still don't know how to manage these novelties. The publisher will find and preserve his role, which is to show how to make a selection, and at the same time he will have to be very attentive to what the readers want. If not, he will find himself out of it. The positions of privilege held during the last centuries, which can basically be reduced to the power of physical distribution, are coming to an end. In ten years, they will not exist. The large publishing groups, who have based their success on distribution, will have to find new competitive opportunities, because everything is about to loosen up.

What is going to happen with copyrighting?
In this new digital era the publisher will no longer sell books, but will lend them as happens with pay TV, with channels that customers will subscribe to... Then, inevitably, the publisher will have to find a new formula for paying the copyright holder. We are used to doing this in a simple way: we pay royalties for every copy sold. It can no longer be done in this way. There are still many problems to be resolved – for example, quantifying the sum of money necessary to pay for copyright. What's more, it's important to realise that these are long-term changes.

Do you think that readers will understand that they have not bought the book, only borrowed it?
We have to be careful. As publisher, the winner will be the one who knows how to work on the content. My objective is to sell, and for that, I do not think the paper book will disappear. Like newspapers, I believe we are at the dawn of the digital age. If I buy the *Financial Times* with a digital subscription, I am also entitled to receive it in paper. The same with a book. If I want to sell the latest book by Haruki Murakami and you buy the physical book, with the price you are paying me for that book you are entitled to other options: you have it in paper, you have it digitally. And that is a type of purchase that will continue to exist, but with both types connected, because the paper book can't do without the digital format in the short term.

And so it will be for hire.
Yes, that's the option for those who don't want to buy the book, but to rent it, like from a library. The reader who says: 'I want a subscription of ten euros a month with which I have access to a selection of books on offer.' And those books can all be new books, for instance, or all romantic fiction, or whatever... These are two different types

of customer, and two different ways of enjoying a book. However it may be that many people would want to buy books by Murakami, García Márquez or Vargas Llosa to keep in their library and rent other books, like historical novels, for entertainment, but not to keep in their homes.

The publisher seems to be like the captain of a ship, and the sea evokes two feelings: solitude and fear. Do you feel either of these feelings at the moment?
The sea inspires a feeling of profound respect, because you know you are in front of some very high waves which could carry you away. It's more or less the same with the world of books. Producing books is easy. The difficult thing is to bring the books to the reader in a clear and intelligible way, and this can only be done through your collections and your brand. As the publisher responsible for a publishing house, this is my objective. The business is built around the figure of the editor — the editors are the heart of the enterprise. My recipe is very simple. It's the only one I know, and it has applied in America and Europe, and up until now it has worked. It has nothing to do with fear or solitude. Fear starts when you begin to forget that and you raise production in order to reach an ephemeral profit, to collect returns... and that is precisely when the sea can overwhelm you.

And so what can we do?
We have to have the guts to renounce the privileges we have acquired and which have maintained our leadership position until now. Now is the moment to reinvent our work. As at all moments of change, this could be painful and uncomfortable, because up to now we controlled everything and one knew all about one's world. Now we have to assume risks, we have to be more curious, to experiment and, above all, be prepared to make mistakes.

What can we do to fight piracy?
Piracy is a very serious thing, very painful, in some countries more than others. But, if I might say so, the pirates are the only ones who know the truth about bestsellers. For an author, to be pirated is almost a satisfaction, because it means you are selling a lot. The pirate is never wrong! It is right to fight it as much as possible, but to tell the truth, the responsibility for piracy (of the digital content above all) rests with the publishers. Music, for instance, has no barriers of language, it used to sell at a very high price, they forced you to buy a CD to end up listening to just one song. At a commercial level, that was without any doubt a stimulus for piracy. We have all – at 12 or 15 years of age – recorded a song from an album to give a cassette tape to a girlfriend. So there is nothing to get frightened about there.

But that's a problem for the publisher.
When piracy has become an economic phenomenon of such importance, it isn't the police who should solve it. An economic solution must be found at the publishing level. For the book, without any doubt, it has been the paperback edition, which hasn't so far been developed to the full in either the Spanish or Italian speaking worlds. The same thing will happen with the digital format. Pirating digital content is much easier. And what is more, if the digital consumer wants something, he is not inclined to adapt to the plans of the publishing house. He wants it now, and if he can get it somewhere else, he pirates it.

That easy?
I am not a pirate, but I download The Beatles onto my iPod if I can't buy them. We have to change our attitude, we have lost our power, and this means we need to tell ourselves to respect the consumer. Respecting them means giving them what they want at the price they want. We need to change our mentality, to know how to construct an

economic structure that can withstand this change. If we are not able to do this, we do not deserve to continue as publishers.

Is all power with the consumer?
No. The power is with both the consumer and the writer. The publisher is an intermediary, a contact between the writer and their public, which has also changed along with their interests. For example, with the digital novel, we are selling much more of the romantic novel imprint, because there are many people who are ashamed to go down the street with a romantic novel. So they read it in digital format. The same as with pornography. Is the publisher losing power? Yes, of course, he has to. It is the author – the one who writes – who has the power, and my job as publisher is to put him in touch with the public. If I don't, the writer will leave me for someone else who knows how to reach the public. In the past, the main problem was to know how to distribute and get to the reader, and this was as true for the big publisher as for the small. Nowadays there is no distinction between the two. Technology has lowered the costs so much that this difference doesn't exist. Now there are no excuses for saying that you cannot achieve success because you are too small and the big groups are destroying you. Now we are going to see who really is worth something.

PERSONAL LIBRARY

1. Salinger, J.D. *The Catcher in the Rye,* Penguin Books, London, 2010
2. Melville, Herman. *Moby Dick,* Ignatius Press, San Francisco, 2011
3. García Márquez, Gabriel. *No One Writes to the Colonel,* Penguin Books, London, 1996
4. Coetzee, J.M. *Disgrace,* Harvill Secker, London, 2010
5. Calvino, Italo. *The Baron in the Trees,* Thomas Learning, Harcourt Brace & Co., New York, 1999
6. Dumas, Alexandre. *The Count of Monte Cristo,* Barnes & Noble, New York, 2004
7. Eggers, Dave. *A Heartbreaking Work of Staggering Genius,* Pan Macmillan, London, 2007
8. Roth, Philip. *American Pastoral,* Vintage, London, 2011
9. Saviano, Roberto. *Gomorrah,* Pan Macmillan, London, 2011
10. Kafka, Franz. *The Trial,* CRW Publishing Limited, Cirencester, UK, 2011

JOAQUÍN DÍEZ-CANEDO

Director of Fondo de Cultura Económica

WHAT I SEE ON THE WEB IS AN ENORMOUS AMOUNT OF NOISE

I interviewed Joaquín Díez-Canedo, a 56-year-old Mexican, at the Wellington Hotel in Madrid. The son of Spanish exiles in Mexico, he has the look of a bullfighter—the air, even, of that great poet of the art of bullfighting, José Bergamín: restrained, discreet and attentive, his eyes firmly fixed on the person speaking to him. His personal biography, which is ample and always related to the publication of books—a vocation that has led him to direct the powerful Fondo de Cultura Económica of Mexico since 2009—converges with a circumstance of radical significance: the legend of his father, the great publisher of the same name, who directed the Joaquín Mortiz publishing house with unique success. It was said of his father that he finely combined humour and paradox with the publisher's trade, losing his composure when, fearful of the shortage of paper, he was forced to submit to the risk of ordering reprints. 'What?! Buy more paper?!' He knew where all of the boxes of unsold books were, and would also launch into a great turmoil of interrogation whenever these boxes would disappear. 'What?! They've been sold?!' This sense of humour with which Díez-Canedo the elder faced his passion for publishing, and the interest he always had in the taste of readers in order to satisfy it, made him, without any doubt, one of the publishing legends of the Spanish language. And his son, now presiding over one of the most important publishing houses in the Hispanic publishing world, the historic Fondo de Cultura, is also an emblem of this changing universe. His position regarding the future is eclectic, as perhaps that of his father's would have been. Someone once said that when there is a storm we must huddle together so the wind won't knock us down.

The legend of your father as an editor is very attractive, as is the reality. Tell me where the spark that made you a publisher comes from.
As is so often the case, I tried to define myself independently from my father, by studying physics. This project did not prosper, because it required more discipline than I have, more brains. Having failed in that attempt, my work opportunities emerged out of the knowledge I had of my father's publishing trade. Instead of giving me *un domingo* ('a Sunday', as it's called in Mexico—that is, some money for my expenses) my father would give me some proofs or a report. Thanks to these jobs from my father, I started to learn the trade. While still at the Science Department, a job as a publisher for the Department of Mathematical Publications appeared. Of all the scientists who were in the department, I was the one who best knew the symbols that are used to mark proofs. I got the job, and from then on many doors opened up for me thanks to my father. It was at the end of the 1970s when I finally confirmed my suspicion that I didn't have a vocation in science. In 1987, almost ten years later, I started working with my father at Mortiz, which at the time was already part of Planeta (as it had been since 1983). I worked with him for seven years, from 1987 until 1993. During this period I got to know another aspect of my father, who was always a man of subtle signals, a man who was far from explicit in his teaching. You had to learn for yourself, by watching, observing. I would come home at night and would see him in the little studio he had, using a typometer to measure quadrats for the publication of an art encyclopaedia, or sometimes correcting proofs—for instance, *The Tin Drum*, by Günter Grass. This was the best example.

Which was published by Mortiz for the first time. Carlos Gerhard was the translator.
Yes, indeed, he was translating for Fondo de Cultura as well. I learned through osmosis, by contagion. But, of course, once I started working at Mortiz I realised what it meant to be a publisher. Mortiz had already traversed the 1960s and 1970s, its glorious years of fame, with a businessman/publisher who had created a prestigious backlist, an entelechy much venerated today.

What lessons did you learn from that traditional publisher who has become a mythical figure?
Acquiring that 'nose', that intangible intuition of the publisher. My father was much more versed in Spanish and Classical literature, his training was much more solid than mine in terms of the history of literature or that of culture in general. But at the end of the day, he would risk relying on his own taste, that very complex thing that develops from an experience, an education, a story, a vision of the world, an epoch, yet nevertheless perceives – or, sometimes, finally manages to perceive – that which is new, original, and particular in a work that could interest more people. I believe he would not have spoken of the publishing market in terms of a reading public, of certain things that one imagines to have understood that would also interest this public. He didn't try to represent anyone, nor to be an example of any theory, but he would recognise something new, interesting, purposeful, different, provocative... That taught me to trust in this thing that is so complicated to maintain, the instinct one has, knowing that one is counting on a very irregular education, full of gaps. Naturally he relied on a group of excellent readers. Now they can be named: Vicente Leñero, Francisco Zendejas, José Agustín, Salvador Elizondo, Sergio Pitol, Bernardo Giner de los Ríos, his nephew, who was always his right-hand man. I've read enough to be able to recognise when something has a certain value, a distinctive value,

because one can't rely on anything else – something that sounds different, that sounds new, interesting, even if it is the continuation of something previous.

As other publishers from North and South America, Spain and other places in Europe, such as Feltrinelli and Gallimard, your father created a legend. What was he like, what was his relationship with books?
My father was a timid and discreet man, perhaps as a result of living in exile in Mexico, along with my grandfather. He was a strong man, sure of himself. He found himself obliged to recognise and affirm his own judgement. Once again, this notion of the publisher who believes in himself, who believes that what he considers good, what he likes, is something valid for many more people. Although he started studying Liberal Arts in Spain, he finished his studies in the Faculty of Philosophy and Liberal Arts of the National Autonomous University of Mexico. He believed in literature and was soon mixing with the Mexicans. Most of society rejected the exiles from Spain, because they were labelled as 'reds', but they were well received by the cultural elite and they made an enormous contribution. All of this, I suppose, created in him a certain insecurity, but he came to terms with it and finally said to himself: 'I think this is worth it.' He succeeded in winning the big prize, which is what lies behind the success of a publishing house. He became very successful in terms of recognition, of publications, but not necessarily in business and economic terms, especially at the end.

Why did he become a publisher?
I think he was almost always a publisher. He started with his brother-in-law, Francisco Giner de los Ríos, in Spain in 1936. They released a little publication called *Floresta* (Grove), and Juan Ramón Jiménez advised them. Many of my grandfather's friends were published there. There are some six or seven issues of *Floresta* from the

first months of the war, before they left for Argentina. When they arrived in Mexico, my father got a job at the Fondo de Cultura in 1942, through my grandfather's connections. In the first general catalogue of Fondo, he appears in the so-called 'technical department', consisting of those who made the books, the actual publishers, not the ones who chose the books, but those who made them. I think it was there, and due to those circumstances, that his vocation as a publisher was defined. He first trained as a typographer and proofreader, and afterwards as a catalogue compiler.

What did you learn from him as a publisher? Nowadays, when you devote yourself to the direction of Fondo, do you ask yourself at some point: 'Would my father have done this in this way?'
I think so, although in reality I recognise myself as having less authority. I have more doubts and I try to rely on other pieces of information rather than on my own taste for things: on what I understand to be the reading public and on what is reflected in the sales of a given collection, of certain books, of certain authors. I try to rely more on sales figures when making publishing decisions than on my own intuition. I am more doubtful of my intuition. It must be said, however, that Fondo is something very different from Joaquín Mortiz. For its editorial decisions, Fondo relies on a structure made up of creators and intellectuals of great weight.

You said that your tastes are different, and that common sense was what characterised your father's decision-making process. Are we saying that you represent, in relation to your father, the two universes of the contemporary reader of the 20th and 21st centuries — that your father was the one with the distinct taste and you are the one with the data?
Yes, one could say that. If we had to present ourselves as the extremes of a spectrum, it would be so.

How do you think the figure of the publisher has changed? How do you see this universe?
In the same way as my father, I consider myself a technician. Back then one had to know the trade of typography, how to make a book on pages. And now it's about something else, it's about what is seen as demand, the trends, and the way in which people gain access to the texts... It has to be done in the best possible way. Apart from this there is the matter of what is being offered to the reader, which is a different thing. But in terms of the trade, I simply believe that what used to be done back then extends itself, prolongs itself, becomes more complex; it incorporates what are called 'new media'. They must be understood; one has to know how to use them, how to take advantage of them and to realise that there are people that demand things in this way. It is a reality. I wouldn't shut myself up in a shell; I wouldn't say, 'I don't understand this, I don't know about this.' I am very much aware of this migration, this enormous technological shift in the actual printing technology. I had to lay out proofs myself, in Ventura Publisher, QuarkXpress, InDesign... All this would have been too much for my father, who would have been tremendously bothered by the new publishing technologies. But for me it's not that hard to understand that even paper itself could be no longer the medium. What I would like to do is to maintain the new ideas, the works and the new authors, no matter how they are disseminated.

Do you think that these technological novelties that put the publisher in a new frame of mind also affect, or will affect, taste, instinct and common sense, or are they unalterable as a basis?
It's difficult to say. I don't think so. I do believe in the author, I believe in the work. The author is a person who lives in a society, who isn't defined as a single thing, who isn't isolated or shut in, even though in the end the writing and the production is a personal matter, intimate and complex, that requires great dedication, because

it continues being so, from *El Quijote* to *In Search of Lost Time*, to *2666*. Obviously it's not something one does in one's free time, while conversing with someone else. A work needs a great deal of personal investment, of mental energy, above all psychological, and of interest in reading the world.

That doesn't change?
It doesn't really change. Of course, now it's legitimised and everyone has the right to think that they can participate. It's a kind of democratisation of creation. Anyone can mention whatever occurs to him or her in 140 characters or more, at whatever moment, about whatever person; but no one can write a book like, say, *Infinite Jest* by David Foster Wallace, or *2666* by Roberto Bolaño, just to name some contemporary books.

But there is something that does change, for example the bookshops. Will they be affected? Will the work of the agents be affected? Do you see the figure of the publisher threatened by piracy, by the competition of the agent, by the competition of Amazon? Do you think that the figure of the publisher has to be considered in a different way at this time?
In a different way, yes. What I see on the web is an enormous amount of noise. Which is to say: who chooses?, who determines? A book is something that takes the author years to conceive, and perhaps publishers are victims of—or are being punished for—a sin of arrogance, which consists in interfering too much in the work of certain authors, in the name of what they suppose to be the author's market. It is true that some need it. There is a gigantic difference between exceptional authors such as Beckett or Joyce, who have total control over what they write, and a series of amateurs who suddenly produce a great novel due to the intervention of a publisher. I think the publisher is always somewhat guilty of interfering with the author,

sometimes too much. Now he is paying for it. The job of the publisher is simply to find books that are more or less finished, and to make them available to the public. As it was said in the discussion we had at the Madrid Book Fair in 2011: 'the one who inserts a book into society is the publisher'; or, 'the author is the book's father, but the book's motor is the publisher.'

However, today there are not only the letters to the editor: now everybody can comment on anything instantly, whatever occurs to him or her. I have no doubt that important things may come out of this as well.

Take the figure of the agent, who tries to be the new publisher. Is this figure a threat, is it a reality, is it an enemy?
It is a threat that in the field of the Spanish language is as old as the Carmen Balcells Agency. She started precisely with *The Green House* in 1967, when she offered to pay everything for Vargas Llosa so that he could dedicate himself to writing. Choosing manuscripts, the actual selection, is but a specific aspect of the publishing business which used to be part of what an editor would do. What do I think is the cause for this shift? It's practically demographic. There are currently many more people who are interested in publicly express-ing how they think things are, many more creators, than personnel at the publishing houses to check through all this material. It was said in the Madrid Book Fair debate: 'not even the agents want to cope with it, the world is overwhelmed.' It's interesting, because it offers the possibility of personal realisation, somewhat reflecting the promise of this modern world and the importance it gives to individuality, which didn't exist before. Everyone feels they have the right to be the author of something. It's just that there are a lot of things that are worthless. Any publisher can see this, because they are repetitions, things that don't have a voice, that don't have a personality. This is precisely what a publisher is able to notice.

There was a kind of segregation, a spin-off in the industry, which consists of the agents, who have also had to assume a part of the royalties (I'm not sure if it was as a result of abuse by the publishers), or to side a bit more with the authors. What is happening now, paradoxically, is that it is they who have to find a place for their authors and who have to make sacrifices in this area.

When I was a publisher, I saw this figure as someone who made choices, whereas the agent would offer them. Now the agent also wants to be the publisher, that is, the one who can choose. Do you think this is a kind of usurpation, an overlapping? And I also ask myself if this is politically correct.

Agents are useful, but actually they are publishers. That is to say, the actual role is that of a publisher – a publisher without a publishing house. I'm going to bring up something for you to think about. What was my father's financial problem? For example, as a new publisher of novels, you publish 45 authors in three years, some have success, and others don't. Personally for you however, this doesn't mean that the successful ones are the best; others might interest you and you will try not to abandon them. I think that what publishers value is not blind obedience to the laws of the market, but being themselves the ones that inform and create the markets. Once again it's a contradiction in economic terms, but it's what everyone would like. What is more valuable to a publisher than having discovered a writer who no one knew and is now mainstream? What is of greater value to Jorge Herralde than having discovered Roberto Bolaño? But, of course, you have another series of authors who are very important to you, who perhaps you think simply need more time, their next novel, but who nonetheless begin to be an economic burden. Because you not only have to finance your new books, but also your reprints, you have to pay royalties, and there comes a time when your successful authors might perceive that your less successful authors are holding them back. I believe this is where the subject of the literary agent comes into play. The same thing will happen to the literary agent, eventually, but for the time being he will take the author's interests into account when the author tells him: 'Listen, I haven't been paid royalties; this publisher ignores me, and while I am a successful author who is selling well, he doesn't answer my calls and delays paying me.' And they migrate towards the top. That is the logic behind the creation of independent publishing houses and their subsequent absorption by the big companies, which are the ones that can really choose the great authors and pay them well. They no longer assume the risks of creating authors; they leave that to this zone of ferment, which is that of the small independent publishers and, sometimes, the literary agencies. But the agencies don't commit themselves, because they have neither inventory, nor paper, nor anything else.

At the moment, the area in which the greatest threat is apparent is in bookshops, especially since the arrival of such giants as Amazon. Do you see the bookseller, not only in Spain or in Latin America, but also throughout the world, being threatened by, or subject to the uncertainty of new technologies and thus becoming obsolete?
Yes, I do see them very much at risk, because they reproduce what a bookseller does: statistical studies, databases, analyses of buying habits, analyses of the buyer's taste, etc. I do believe that for someone like you or me, a bookshop is much more pleasant as a social space, but perhaps there are people who are accustomed to finding the things that interest them on the screen of a computer, without having to go out of their house.

Is it a generational question?
I think so. Or it will be. I'm also surprised by something I'm see-ing—I'm not sure whether it also occurs here, but it can be seen in

Mexico—which might be a result of a sense of nostalgia or fear: the wish to instil in your children the same ideas that you have. That is to say, you do not only transmit what you believe are basic principles and attitudes towards life, but also things like this: we would like our children to go to bookshops, because we find it interesting being there, seeing other people. However, there will be generations that won't need it.

What do you feel when you make this prediction?
I think that what is necessary, especially with regard to our profession, is to understand and to offer other possibilities. People have to have access to these works and their authors. It seems that for the time being, the new technologies don't reflect the work and the author in such an exact, or in such a complete way as a book does, in the sense of reading it from cover to cover, of an author signing it for you. Not yet.

They will invent it.
Exactly, nothing prevents us from thinking that they can invent it, and if they invent it, why should we insist on it having a certain form and not another, if the experience will be the same and it will generate the same thing in people in terms of a vital experience? By the same token we needn't insist on paper, on cutting down trees even though they have been planted, in other words, on recycled paper.

Wouldn't your father have said: 'How are we going to buy paper for reprinting now?'
Yes, indeed. Back then it was a dilemma: whether to print 1,000 copies of *Terra Nostra*, by Carlos Fuentes, or 1,000 copies of six more titles one sixth the size of *Terra Nostra*. I don't know if he had this specific problem, but in effect it was a dilemma that technology now

simplifies or eliminates. For example, for Fondo de Cultura, which has such an extensive catalogue and thinks and believes that the entire catalogue is important, new technologies offer a great solution. I can print 10,000 copies of a children's book in colour that we sell a lot of, or 25,000 copies of *The Labyrinth of Solitude*, by Octavio Paz. But I can also print 300 copies of the two volumes of Gilbert Height's book on the classic tradition that Juan Almela translated for the Fondo, a very important book for which there is a reliable demand of 400 copies in Mexico. And all this without financially compromising the company, by keeping them in stock, because they are copies that I sell each year without variation.

Is that the best way?
Printing on demand? At Fondo we have a historic catalogue of many diverse titles, around 8,600; but in 2009 we sold at least one copy each of some 5,000 or so titles. I would like to continue selling up until the last copy requested of me — and that, with printing on demand, is perfectly feasible. Technology allows me to do it without having to sacrifice the rest of my books. I believe without doubt that it's the best of all possible worlds.

In other words, you are receptive to novelty.
Absolutely.

Do you see any sign of alarm, something that worries you about the current situation?
I'm worried, for example, about having a warehouse. It is difficult for a publishing house to be self-sufficient. It's very complicated for a publisher with fewer than 150 authors in the catalogue to make a good number of sales, to get a good distribution, to maintain some of their offices... It's complicated to grow as a publisher. In general, once you have 250 titles, the problem arises of those that don't sell

so well, that hinder you financially, and the ones that sell go elsewhere. It's like a football team with one genius, or a second division or third division team that has great players. I think it's something that happens everywhere. But I think in the business of paper books it's still economically feasible for publishers to do this. I do believe that now certain technologies require a very hefty investment. Or at least some people have taken the lead in such a way that it's very complicated to compete with them. That's what Amazon did with the e-book. They were the first to create good hardware that provides good support, they have worked very hard on their distribution and electronic commerce platforms, they have completed it with a series of products that are not books, and now it's very complicated to compete with them. I believe that other economic agents can exist other than the publishers who can take some of the load, or who can displace them or threaten them a bit. Finally, one can't be so arrogant as to think that publishers are an alien, Martian and very rare species. They are people who are well read, with a certain taste and with a certain family history. One has to think of this idea in *Outliers: The Story of Success*, by Malcolm Gladwell. There isn't anyone exceptional who doesn't have a background that justifies it, an exceptional family. There are few literary publishers—who are, as it were, the elite class of the publishing world—but that doesn't mean that one can't think that other people from other backgrounds might also have good ideas in this area.

Under these circumstances, how do you see the future of a giant like Fondo de Cultura?
We have very important support from the Mexican government, something that began with José Vasconcelos at the beginning of the 20th century. The intention was to put the recently literate reader in contact with the great authors of Western culture, to familiarise the people with the classics: Plato, Plotinus, Homer, but also Dante,

Goethe, Tagore... The Mexican state has always understood the task of giving support to culture, including subsidising culture, which is what Fondo has. The tradition of Fondo, since I've known it, understands that this must be passed on to the readers by trying to keep all the books that have at some point been considered important or useful within their reach. Technology is a great help in keeping this great catalogue alive. What we are talking about is precisely the transmission of a very important tradition which, of course, can be covered with ten or 12 books that are fundamental, but which has an enormous scope of nuances and possibilities. Within these margins, in these strange works, is where new ideas or the possibility of transcending things finally arise. If they are conserved, here we have this cultural heritage, this great corpus, which people can hold in their hands so they will remember and maintain this great tradition. And now new technology allows for this in an economic and financially efficient way. I think this is what is fundamental.

And piracy?

Fortunately, hackers are not interested in books that have little demand. Piracy, in part, has a good reason to exist, which is the fact that publishers in general have a lot of difficulties having all their books in all places at all times. Technology offers the possibility of having more books in more places for longer periods of time. The promise of meeting 100 per cent of demand is getting nearer. If you would like to print all 350 pages of *One Hundred Years of Solitude* (which will get damaged), on A4 with your printer, with your toner, and then bind them... what a bore! If they can give you a book for just a little more and you can have it even if you are in Aracataca (where I think Gabriel García Márquez's books probably don't get to – or where, at best, those are the only books to arrive), why would you hack anything at all? I do believe that the hacking of complete books is a criminal business of another sort: they are small subtractions from the print runs of publishing houses; but in this aspect, technology favours you once again, because nowadays it's very cheap to print. Before there was the very important economic factor of scale, which has now practically disappeared.

Will this facility in publishing be the end of selection, of choice?
I think that there may be people who are not aware that they are reading trash; it's obvious. I'm sorry to say that I think there is a lot of literature that contributes little, that is a repetition; there is an amount of knowledge that in reality is pseudo-knowledge, a fraud, superstition... I think there is a lot of fraud in self-help, the motivational. There are a lot of people who are not aware that there are a whole lot of things that won't help them. But those who are interested will search for selectivity, someone who will guide them, who will fortify them, who will tell them what is good and what isn't. This is what the prestigious publishers do, and they do exist. They all have the right to feel proud of their name. There is a social reality: the most important authors aren't necessarily the ones that sell the most. There are two types of selection: that which everyone wants and everyone comments on, and then some things that fewer people probably comment on, but which seem to contribute more ideas, more solutions, more ways of coming to terms with things and with life.

Are readers changing? Have you yourself changed as a reader?
Of course readers are changing. This idea that, 'I only know that I know nothing' is an affirmation that is becoming more and more true, at least in terms of what is being written, and we tend to read less and less because it's getting harder to find the time. The fact that novelties proliferate all over the place doesn't seem negative to me. Of course, each one thinks that such a quantity of titles will necessarily compromise the sale of each, for a logical and elementary reason. I think it has to be so.

I was talking about the reader.
Of course, there will be fewer possibilities, but it is possible to see these hierarchical mechanisms continuing to function: the agents, the publishing houses, and the literary supplements. Everybody still reads *The New York Review of Books* or *Babelia*, or takes notice of Jorge Herralde or of Fondo... In short, everyone continues to need these institutions and authorities to tell them: 'Well, there are a thousand things to read, but it would be good if you tried to read these ones because they are more interesting.' It will be more complicated, noisier, but one can't do without this, because the experience of navigation is tiresome. Although surfing the web interminably might produce a certain addiction, I imagine that the triviality of the little things that are constantly being said transmits a sensation of loss, of confusion, of exhaustion, of fatigue, and it is then that one goes back to saying: 'Well, maybe I would do best to keep to these few things I've been recommended.' Consider how we continue reading the Greeks, who wrote 2,500 years ago, how they have been referred to thousands of times and are on display everywhere, and nevertheless we continue going back to them because they expressed themselves well, because they give us clarity and because they teach us things we didn't know.

The other day I happened to come across someone walking down the street reading Plutarch.
Why do the classics of the Spanish publishing house Gredos continue to sell in the newsstands? They have a certain prestige. Even though there is an appearance of wealth in this great noise, it is exhausting and complicates things, and people get lost, confused, and at some point say: 'Who will tell me where I'm going, who will show me the way to go?' I think that this is, in general, the task of the publisher.

What is your suitcase like, is it very heavy?
Not very – I try not to overload it. I buy at airports on my departure.

There are very good bookshops in the airports of first world cities. That is where I supply myself. I buy all of my favourite English-writing authors in pocket-book format at airports: such as Ian McEwan, Kazuo Ishiguro, Haruki Murakami—well, I've read Murakami in English—and I read them on the plane.

What would your father say about these times?
I think they would make him feel uncomfortable, but really only because he was a man of a different generation. My father was a conservative man, politically as well—he was not reactionary or anything of the sort, but, yes, conservative, in the sense that he thought that there are few things that are worth something. However, he was a great publisher of novelties. I'm not going to decipher my father; I would have to try to write his biography.

PERSONAL LIBRARY

1. Anonymous. *The Arabian Nights: Tales from a Thousand and One Nights*, Modern Library, New York, 2001

2. Voltaire. *Candide: Or Optimism*, Penguin Classics, London, 2009

3. Darwin, Charles. *The Origin of Species*, Barnes & Noble, New York, 2003

4. Dostoyevsky, Fyodor. *The Brothers Karamazov*, Penguin Classics, London, 2003

5. Broch, Hermann. *The Sleepwalkers*, Vintage Books, London, 1996

6. Malraux, André. *The Human Condition*, Vintage Books, London, 1990

7. Faulkner, William. *The Sound and the Fury*, Vintage Books, London, 2009

8. García Márquez, Gabriel. *One Hundred Years of Solitude*, Harper Perennial Modern Classics, New York, 2006

9. Molina, Enrique. *Una sombra donde sueña Camila O'Gorman*, Editorial Seix Barral, Barcelona, 1983

10. Hughes, Ted. *Gaudete*, Harper & Row, New York, 1977

INGE FELTRINELLI

President of Feltrinelli Editore

BEFORE, PUBLISHERS WERE THE PSYCHIATRISTS
AND EVEN THE LOVERS OF AUTHORS

Inge Feltrinelli, President of Feltrinelli, is without a doubt, the *grande dame* of European publishing. Now her son Carlo, CEO of Feltrinelli, who shares his mother's enthusiasm, steps into the Spanish publishing world – as a result of an agreement with Jorge Herralde, director of Anagrama – and in a few years he will take charge of this mythical publishing house. However, we were not visiting Inge at her office in Milan to talk about this, but about the legacy she received from her late husband, Giangiacomo Feltrinelli, who suffered a violent death while handling a bomb in 1972, in the years when he combined his arrests as a revolutionary with his work as a publisher. The memory of this event casts a shadow over Inge's smiles and laughter during our conversation. It is the same shadow that we see on the DVD she launched on her 80th birthday, when she was the recipient of all kinds of honours and tributes. Our conversation has to do with this legacy as well as with the future of books, the theme of this series of interviews. Inge's office is full of memorabilia from past years, from her contacts all over the world; but also from an aspect of her life that she herself is now happy to highlight: her years as a photographer. The years when she took a portrait of a drunken Hemingway in his Cuban ranch or surprised Greta Garbo blowing her nose in a chic New York street. Inge Feltrinelli was born in Germany, and she met her husband-to-be during a photo-shoot. Now, all these memories, shrouded in the melancholy of Giangiacomo's absence, lie behind this universe that Carlo, her son, keeps afloat and on course.

How do you feel in a world that has changed so much?
You told me old friends like Peter Mayer, Antoine Gallimard or Michael Krüger would also be participating in this series. I heard their names, and thought of them as old dinosaurs. But, in fact, I am the oldest dinosaur of all. And it is true that our world has changed a lot; we have e-books now and we must confront them as something new which sets a direction. They are here, they are the future; but I also believe that paper books are a unique product. Because they are cheap and because they are like those projects that cannot be improved; we could even say that books are sensual objects; we can smell the paper, see the graphics, touch them, and even write on them. There is no way books are going to disappear.

How do you see e-books?
As interesting toys – for example, in universities. But the paper book is an object that will stay, the same way bicycles have not disappeared with the introduction of cars, or radios with the appearance of television. Books will continue to exist; books will always be profitable. We have opened more than 100 bookshops, and that is a sign of the optimism that encourages us to keep working.

These bookshops are an unusual enterprise in today's world.
There are many regions in Italy where people feel the need for large bookshops; in our country there are many paperback publishers who offer quality products: Faulkner, Hemingway, Sciascia, Eugenio Montale... And the bookshops are full of people who look for this kind of literature, for copies that are cheaper than a pizza. Books are very cheap!

Books continue, publishers have to change...
I have seen the big publishers change a lot. I have met the giants:
Gaston and Claude Gallimard, Alfred A. Knopf, Paul Flamand...
I knew Giulio Einaudi, Valentino Bompiani, and Giangiacomo... Back
then, Feltrinelli belonged to a new generation and he was no ordinary man either. Few books were published then, agents did not
exist, the publisher was the agent, the banker, the nurse, the secretary of an author. The publisher was everything. It was a different
world. They were the psychiatrists and, in some cases, the lovers.
A good publisher brought out 40 good books, not 150 or 200. The
world has changed. They were people who loved books passionately.
When Heinrich Maria Ledig-Rowohlt noticed that the translation of
Vladimir Nabokov's *Lolita* was inadequate, he locked himself in a
hotel with four translators and produced a translation that satisfied
him. It was a different world.

Is there less quality in this world?
It is a different quality. There have always been waves – good times
and bad times. There are the years when a Gabriel García Márquez
might appear. We were the ones who started publishing García
Márquez and Mario Vargas Llosa in Italy. We published all the great
Latin Americans.

**The relationship between author and publisher has also changed. You
had García Márquez and, in spite of the loyalty you felt towards each
other, he left.**
García Márquez had his first success in a foreign language here. We
sold 300,000 copies of *One Hundred Years of Solitude*. After that
he became very famous and very expensive and his agent wanted
a lot of money. Feltrinelli was going through a crisis after Giangiacomo's death; we wanted to reprint all his works, but we did not
have enough money to do it. In spite of our great mutual respect and

friendship we could not continue working with him, we were up to our necks in problems.

There was a time when agents did not exist. How was it back then? And today, how has the relationship with the writer changed?
There are many more writers now. A publisher cannot be father and boss anymore: the editor as a protagonist who does it all himself. In Feltrinelli, for example, we worked as a team, the way Giangiacomo wanted. Each editor was responsible for a different section, but the decisions were taken by the whole group. Now, Carlo receives a report from each editor, they all have their own creative criteria and have to defend their choices. I remember an anecdote Alfred A. Knopf once told me: an editor presented his proposal, 'This book is not bad.' And he answerd 'What do you mean, not bad? Either it is good or it is bad. Would you eat an egg if they told you it was not bad?' Anyway, today it is practically impossible to be close friends with an author, to be intimate and talk one to one. With some it may work, but not with all. What is more, nowadays the agents are the ones who keep in contact with the writers, they do everything. But the beautiful part of publishing is precisely the contact with the author. There was a time when it was possible to fall in love with the writer, with the person. Today that seldom happens. A long time ago, an author would arrive in Milan alone, without an agent, to meet the publisher. That is not necessary anymore. The agent takes care of all that and the author simply receives a copy of his published book at home. It is a sort of bigamy or threesome. And some friendships may last a lifetime, but divorce also occurs.

How do you see the figure of Giangiacomo Feltrinelli today?
Giangiacomo belonged to the younger post-war generation, of young intellectuals with left-wing ideals who suffered the trauma of not having fought in the war against Franco. He was part of a group of

anti-fascists that wanted to cleanse Italy of Fascism; they wanted a new country, and he had the ideas, the money and the political predisposition to try to do it. This publishing house was created with the desire to change this country, with the commitment to publish new authors.

Feltrinelli said that the publisher must not, should not catechise because, in a sense, the publisher does not know.
I do not agree, that is an exaggeration. After half a century of working here, I know some things; for example, teamwork is very important. Before, the publisher was the main character, the person who read the book; today it does not work like that. I have also learned that friendship is fundamental: there are publishers, like Mayer or Krüger, who call us and inform us about books that are 'for you.' In the publishing world a great amount of passion and rigour are necessary, but so is luck.

Giangiacomo also said that a publisher should try to change ('change, change and change') society. Has it changed?
Of course it has changed. There were no readers in Italy. When Giangiacomo died we had seven bookshops, now we have 103. The market is much larger, because young people finally are starting to read more, in spite of PlayStation and Google. Fifty per cent of Italians do not buy a book in their whole lives. But there is an 11 per cent of great readers who always read, just as in Germany and France. When Giangiacomo began the situation was much worse. In half a century we have stimulated this country.

I read somewhere that you transformed pain into energy. I wanted to ask you about pain. The pain caused by the World War, by your husband's death...
I try to forget bad things straight away, it is a healthy rejection of

pain. I always talk about what is ahead of me. The past does not interest me any longer. As Giuseppe Ungaretti wrote, we all live on memory; everything is memory, but I try to move on, I am a child-like optimist.

There are some important episodes in your memory: the picture of a drunken Hemingway, the picture of Greta Garbo blowing her nose in the middle of a New York avenue, your decision to carry on with the publishing house after your husband's death...
I do the same things now that I used to when I was 18. My priority was to earn money, because my family was very poor, but I also wanted to find excellence in life. I am fascinated by the giants in literature, in life; extraordinary people who are very rare. Today I am still searching for excellence, human, intellectual, political... I want to achieve the maximum.

And that is why you fell in love with Feltrinelli?
Feltrinelli was beyond category. He was not a typical left-wing man, he was not a typical millionaire, he was not a typical intellectual. He was quite exceptional, impossible to classify.

A German Romantic, according to you.
Our friend Jorge Brega said: 'He died because of his tormented co-herence.' It is a wonderful definition: Giangiacomo was tormented by his own coherence with himself.

The mystery of his violent death remains.
He was too dangerous for Italy; he was clever, he spoke five languages, he even knew how to speak Spanish well. I always spoke with him in German. He was no ordinary man, but he made a mistake. He did not understand that his idea of changing Italy was mistaken, although maybe at the end he did understand. He was convinced that

Operazione Gladio existed, an organisation created by a type of Italian CIA led by military men who were against democracy. Giangiacomo wanted to reunite a group of veteran partisans against it. I thought he was wrong and we argued a lot.

You say you argued a lot, especially after his trip to Cuba in 1967. We can read it on your face in the movie they made to celebrate your 80th birthday.
Yes, because Giangiacomo wanted to organise a coup as a result of the situation; it was preposterous, he acted with a childish romanticism, it was madness.

There are very revealing letters of what happened in Cuba when he met Castro.
When he first met Castro, Giangiacomo was arrogant towards him; Castro liked that, because he was used to earnest and servile followers. And Feltrinelli reproached him that he did not let people live freely. Castro was furious, but he liked Giangiacomo all the same, because he saw he was not afraid of him.

You talk of dreams. What has been your best realised dream?
My son. I always say this, in all modesty, because it seldom happens that the son of a publisher assumes control of his parents' publishing house. Many great publishers have had no children. The world of publishing is so restless, so difficult and complex that it cannot be passed on from parent to child; the Fiat company can be inherited, but a publishing house cannot, it is different, it would not work. And, that a son should work with his mother is impossible. And this dream has come true. I have many dreams, I would like greater success for my authors, I would like at least ten Nobel Prizes before I die.

PERSONAL LIBRARY

1. Pasternak, Boris. *Doctor Zhivago*, Vintage Books, New York, 2011
2. Lowry, Malcolm. *Under the Volcano*, Penguin Modern Classics, London, 2007
3. Grass, Günter. *The Tin Drum*, Mariner Books, New York, 2010
4. García Márquez, Gabriel. *One Hundred Years of Solitude*, Harper Perennial Modern Classics, New York, 2006
5. Guimarães Rosa, João. *The Devil to Pay in the Backlands*, Knopf, New York, 1971
6. Scott Fitzgerald, F. *Tender is the Night*, Alma Books, Richmond, UK, 2012
7. De Beauvoir, Simone. *The Second Sex*, Vintage Books, London, 2011
8. Hemingway, Ernest. *The Sun Also Rises*, Thinking Ink Media, Brighton, UK, 2011
9. Di Lampedusa, Giuseppe Tomasi. *The Leopard*, Vintage Books, London, 2010
10. Tabucchi, Antonio. *Pereira Declares*, New Directions, New York, 1997

ANTOINE GALLIMARD

President and CEO of Éditions Gallimard

THE DANGER IS NOT IN THE DIGITAL BOOK,
IT IS IN THE FREE BOOKS

There is a miniature ship somewhere in Antoine Gallimard's splendid office in the publishing house that his grandfather Gaston founded 100 years ago.

There are also the books of La Pléiade, the impeccable collection of classics this publisher created 'which has shaped French literary criteria', as it is put in the monumental biography of its founder by Pierre Assouline.

And it is of course the atmosphere that Antoine himself has created, as head of this ocean liner of European culture, which has continued to make Gallimard a publishing beacon of the 20th century, now ready to cut a very difficult passage through the oceanic challenges of the 21st century. He is ready and willing, he says.

He is a sailor. Antoine leaves this office, just near his home, where he has been photographed by Daniel Mordzinski, and goes alone to the sea, to read, to update his instruction manual for keeping his ship on course.

We sit in front of this sailor in his sober office, from whose walls the Pléiade looks down at us.

How does a great publisher see the future of the book?
First of all, there are no great publishers, but simply publishers, it doesn't matter if they are big or small. I'm not worried about the place of the book in the future. I'm sure that it will still be extremely important. The digital book, far from being the end of the book, is a new opportunity for it. A book is not only an alignment of characters, a layout, some chapters; the digital book doesn't do more than give a new body, a new weight to the traditional book. The digital book, like photography, allows great flexibility: different formats, unlimited reprints. So it is an opportunity to enrich the catalogue and to keep books alive. I believe the future of the book depends on the publishers and the writers. To exercise this profession, it is not only necessary to love literature, but to love writers, to love people, and the public. It is a job that arises from the desire to share secret universes through the book. Mario Vargas Llosa said it very well in his Nobel speech: 'I tell stories to make life better.' We will always need stories to make life better. That's why I believe that the book has a brilliant future.

Were you an optimist before all this or just from the moment when everybody began to be pessimistic?
I think one must be voluntarily optimistic. The thing that has worried me over these last years has not been the appearance of the digital book, but the new way of searching for satisfaction in the communities of adolescents, who have added to the time they dedicate to watching television a whole plethora of activities and social practices on the Internet, in such a way that they spend less and less time reading.

And is it possible that the young will go back to books?
It will always be difficult to protect oneself from life's difficulties. They are there, and one has to confront them. The question would be to know if our civilisation and our love of reading, all this culture of the written word that we have inherited from our ancestors, will suffer a kind of regression to the Middle Ages and convert us into monks in monasteries, or if, on the contrary, we are going to know how to address the general public. We needn't fear that a certain kind of a reader will disappear: there are still very demanding kinds of writer, with great success and big sales. But there has always been a large distance between writers like Jorge Luis Borges or Octavio Paz and the literature that 'reaches' the general public. These things aren't fate. We could ask ourselves if this larger public is going to dedicate itself exclusively to Facebook or to continue reading. I'm convinced that there will always be readers. Literature has always been something precious: extremely fragile whilst at the same time wonderfully resistant. No, we don't have to fear for its disappearance. We have already seen how it has survived the rise of new forms of communication; but at the same time, we cannot expect it to expand. A lot of ink has been spilled concerning the evolution of the publishing world towards the world of business, about how publishing houses like Planeta, Hachette or Bertelsmann have been buying and selling other companies. But these big movements of capital bear no relation, strictly speaking, to the world of the book, with the culture of the book.

Pierre Assouline's book about your grandfather shows that the pre-occupations of today were the same as the worries of the past. He was worrying about whether or not he should publish popular literature and he created the Black Series. Are you worried about the relationship between the industry and your personal conception of the book?
The problems have not really changed since the beginning of the

20th century. My grandfather had no doubts about publishing very commercial books alongside other much more demanding books, such as the poetry of Federico García Lorca or Paul Valéry's essays. The important thing was to know how it would be possible to combine the publishing of popular books and the publishing of books of quality. And to risk a decision. My grandfather didn't want to publish Georges Simenon in the Pléiade, even though André Gide was in favour. It was a mistake on his part, which I corrected. On the other hand, Louis-Ferdinand Céline was published in the former Pléiade, even though he was an anti-Semite and a provocateur. It was a difficult choice and a very brave one. In the role of publisher you have to know how to love, but at the same time you have to know how to choose. You shouldn't to put limits on literary taste. One always has to search, as a fisherman searches, but at the same time you have to know and allow the tides to come, instead of trying to attract them.

Your grandfather had enormous authority and dominated all sectors of the publishing industry. What are the differences between his role and the role of the publisher today?
In my grandfather's time, the bookshop had a very important function, there were a lot of independent family-owned publishing houses: the world of the book was really like a small village. Today, the market rules, and we find large chains, big stores, very few independent publishers, a large concentration of powerful groups and fewer and fewer bookshops. Fortunately, publishing houses are not building airplanes, and they can regain balance more easily when they are confronted with the problems of the market and distribution, the size of the productive enterprise doesn't make a fundamental difference. The strength of Gallimard has its roots in the fact that it is a publishing house of writers. André Malraux, Octavio Paz, and Jorge Luis Borges have recommended books to us; writers such as Mario Vargas Llosa still discover writers for us.

Gallimard has kept its independence for an entire century. How has it succeeded in doing so?
There are different factors that have protected this publishing house in times of danger: the respect for quality, public opinion, even the concern of politicians like Mitterrand. There has been a general movement of sympathy for our literary task, for a publishing house that has represented something important throughout its history and continues to do so now.

Does Gallimard have the same intellectual and cultural objectives now that we are in the middle of the digital revolution?
The digital revolution is a technological revolution that is based on the speed with which we can grasp the content. The most important thing is to know whether this revolution is really going to transform the behaviour of the reader or the imagination of the writer. I don't believe that's going to happen, just as radio and television haven't transformed anything in this sense. That is why the danger does not lie in the digital book; as I said before, the digital edition is an opportunity. The real danger is the free book. It is not a question of blaming the Internet but piracy. We are now working to create a digital collection that will be attractive to young people, and that will not be too expensive. Gallimard has entered into legal proceedings against service providers such as Orange, so that they cease hosting sites where people can illegally upload books from our publishing house. And we have succeeded in getting them to close the sites. But at the same time Orange has attacked us in the name of free access. As President of the SNE (National Syndicate of French Publishers), I am actually fighting for the rights of digital exploitation and for obtaining a law that secures control of the prices for digital books, as much to preserve the value of the book, for the creation, for the editing as to protect the booksellers and the writers.

Music and cinema have been strongly affected by piracy. Do you believe that the book business is better equipped to cope with piracy than film or music?
The book is better armed than music because, in its essence, it is not so immaterial. The book appeals to more senses: to the touch with its format, to the smell with its paper, to the sight... and, historically, the intermediary is the bookseller.
In France, we are lucky that we can still count on very good booksellers – it is the opposite in the United Kingdom, for example: there the bookseller has nearly disappeared. The world of music never realised the danger it faced, but the book has arrived to the digital world later than music. Even politicians, the mass media and public opinion have registered an awareness of the danger. Now we are trying to make the market as extensive and attractive as possible, but without failing to fight against piracy.

But there is a sector which thinks that culture must be free of charge.
No doubt about it. Not only in France, everywhere.

And how can you fight for the book in the digital medium?
It is important to build a legislative framework that helps sustain the market. If publishers stop fighting amongst themselves over book prices, they can create a new market to settle into. Until now, commercial politics have been directed mainly by the big chains, such as FNAC. Publishers must secure more say in commercial politics. And the European Union must come to an agreement, once and for all, on imposing measures with respect to piracy as harsh as those against paedophilia, for example. It must be accepted that piracy exists and must be punished. This will be done, it is a matter of time.

Do you think that European opinion is ready to accept such unpopular measures?

No, not yet I think, it is probably too soon. But I see it happening over the next 20 years.

What is your perception, as a traditional publisher, of the current digital book market?
For the moment, our experience in this sector is very limited. In the USA, the digital market has begun to be very important. In France, up to now it is less than 1 per cent. We find in it very little literature and hardly any art books. Nevertheless, we have digitised our list so that the works are more available, which also makes it easier for us to react when the time of publication arrives. In 2007, the first public machine for the 'express book' was installed in the USA, which provides the user with the printing and binding of a book *à la carte* in a matter of minutes. Without doubt, the digital book makes a lot of things easier—for example, returns from bookshops create a difficult problem for the publisher, but the digital book solves the problem of storage.

Could it happen that, like in a Hitchcock film, we are being diverted by our worries about the digital book from other matters more crucial for the future of the book?
The digital book worries us because it could imply, above all, the disappearance of the natural mediators between the reader and the writer. And we are afraid that this will bring forth a real up-heaval, a radical change in the world of the book. That there will be no more need for publishers or booksellers. In fact, I think the opposite, that it can prompt a return to certain traditional values, a rejection of the idea that our lives revolve around money, in the same way that there are already alternative movements against fast food of very bad quality or against compulsive consumerism, especially now that we are in the middle of an economic crisis. This is what I am betting on.

The people around you refer to you as the captain of a ship. For people who are not sailors like you, a ship can evoke the idea of loneliness and fear. Do you feel this loneliness sometimes, or this fear, in the cultural world of today? Are we in a moment when such feelings would be legitimate?

The maritime image is apt for two reasons. First, because I like sailing the coasts and seas, I like to discover peoples and landscapes. Second, because the crew is fundamental to me. It can happen that there are nights when I can't sleep, so I get up and read a book; but during the day, the presence of the crew reassures me. I have friends everywhere who are sailing the ship of the world of the book, I maintain with them a relationship that is warm, hospitable and generous.

A veteran Spanish journalist, Jesús de la Serna, says that the captain always eats alone in his cabin.

I like that too, being alone. There is nothing more important than to allow moments for oneself. For example, moments of reading.

A publishing house that has passed from your grandfather to your father, and then to you. How much does tradition weigh here?

Our tradition is to discover and publish a book for its intrinsic quality. And to preserve one's tradition, sometimes you have to wring its neck – if not, you will be converted into a caricature of your own history. That's why Gallimard hasn't been afraid to publish at the same time authors who are very different from each other; from the Surrealists, the *nouveau roman* or François Mauriac, to contemporary authors.

Is there a word that you would use to define your relationship with the world of publishing?

I would say, patience.

PERSONAL LIBRARY

1. Céline, Louis-Ferdinand. *Journey to the End of the Night*, Alma Books, Richmond, UK, 2012
2. Proust, Marcel. *In Search of Lost Time*, Modern Library, New York, 2003
3. Zweig, Stefan. *Beware of Pity*, Pushkin Press, London, 2011
4. Choderlos de Laclos, Pierre. *Dangerous Liaisons*, Penguin Books, London, 2010
5. Nabokov, Vladimir. *Lolita*, Penguin Classics, London, 2012
6. De Cervantes, Miguel. *Don Quixote*, Vintage Classics, London, 2007
7. Cossery, Albert. *The Lazy Ones*, New Directions, New York, 1952
8. Hardy, Thomas. *The Mayor of Casterbridge*, HarperCollins, London, 2011

JORGE HERRALDE
Founder and Director of Editorial Anagrama

JORGE HERRALDE AND THE CONSTRUCTION OF TASTE

The first time I met Jorge Herralde in his office 20 years ago, he was surrounded by manuscripts, looking at papers inundating the floor with the expression of someone who balances both shyness and serenity with the excitement that comes from the quest, the at times obsessive impatience to discover what he loves. Steadfastly with the help – which in his case cannot be ignored – of his wife, Lali, he has built a universe of books which have his mark; that is to say, the stamp which is not only that of his authors, all of them so diverse, but also that of Anagrama. In today's publishing world, this tradition represents a kind of miracle, since it is uncommon, under present-day circumstances, to find catalogues that closely resemble the intellectual profile of the publisher. Anagrama therefore represents the unfolding of the biography of Herralde's personal taste. The combination includes discrimination, enthusiasm and an eagerness to discover, and also a desire to be authentic, knowing how difficult it is to take a chance on that 'legitimate rarity' inspired by his reading of a line by René Char, and which he repeats like a personal motto every time you ask him a question that might require clarification: 'Develop your legitimate rarity.' And he is indeed rare, Herralde, a rarity; he isn't someone you can define with one stroke of the brush. In fact, you would have to read his whole catalogue in order to define him. And it is a good thing to read this interview, to know how this man with so many years of service behind him sees the future, who in five years time, when he will be 80, will share the adventure of publishing with Feltrinelli, a company also built from personal taste, from the raging desire to publish in order to understand. I asked Herralde: 'Is this profession worth it?' To which he replied: 'I wouldn't know how to do anything else'.

Many years of service, right?
I started in the 1960s. After some projects or fantasies that never really gelled, I decided to become a publisher in September 1967. I went to Paris, spent a week visiting all the publishing houses that interested me, and in April 1969 the first books came out.

What drew you to this trade?
Reading, I think, as with all literary publishers, the same as with authors. And from there, to try and transmit one's enthusiasms. Publishing is basically a passionate affair. In Spain in those days, in the 1960s, there were continents to be discovered, thanks largely to the censorship. Many relevant books had been published in Latin America, interestingly the best publishing houses there had been established or run by exiled Spaniards, from Losada to López Llausás, at Sudamericana, to Joaquín Mortiz, run by Díez-Canedo, the son of the great literary critic; notable intellectuals also entered Fondo de Cultura. All this was very important.

For years, owing to censorship, we had to read many novels that had been translated in Argentina or in Mexico. Now I am constantly being asked about Spanish translations in interviews and conferences in Latin America: 'They're not easy to understand, there's a lot of slang.' This is especially true of very contemporary novels with a lot of dialogue, not with essays or other types of novels. My answer is: 'Get used to it.' I read Argentine translations in my youth where, aside from verb tenses, there was also a whole list of words that were different — *el saco*, *la pollera*, *la pileta* [Latin American Spanish for 'jacket', 'dress', and 'basin'] — but then, with a bit of goodwill, you could soon understand.

You said the word 'enthusiasm', which is a word that defines you well, but how does one maintain enthusiasm in a trade where there are so many ups and downs, where there are disappointments because authors stay, leave, or demand more from the literary agents who foul up the arena?

I don't know why. It must be some genetic anomaly, but the enthusiasm persists. In effect, this is a very bizarre, very passionate trade, with a very particular relationship with the authors, and it's subject to many sudden shocks. These shocks, as you, having been a publisher know very well, cause deep wounds. All the same, one must overcome them and continue forward.

And there is always the incentive that comes from discovering new authors, or to be more precise, because the word 'discover' is a bit emphatic, from recognising that the manuscript of an unknown writer is very good, that you think it is very good. I mention this thing about recognition, because a great English publisher, Diana Athill, has now published *Stet: An Editor's Life* at Trama editorial. I read it and liked it very much, and she is more in favour of the concept of recognition than that of discovery. So am I.

You are at a culminating moment of your career as a publisher; you've been in this for...

Forty-two years. The first book, which for all intents and purposes marks the birth of a publishing house, came out on 23 April 1969.

Which was your first book?

There were several, almost simultaneously: *Details*, by Hans Magnus Enzensberger, and a book on Pierre Choderlos de Laclos and *Dangerous Liaisons*, by Roger Vailland. They were very well received by the critics. They were on display in the 1969 Madrid Book Fair, and *Triunfo* magazine published a very enthusiastic half-page article about the two books. The journalist Juby Bustamante also conducted my first interview as a publisher for *Madrid* newspaper, an unexpected and joyful surprise. And in Catalan we created an ephemeral collection of texts published in Spanish in Latin America which were difficult to find here, but whose authors and books had had a great impact on me, such as *L'ofici de viure* by Cesare Pavese, considered then one of the most important Italian writers, and *Baudelaire*, by Jean-Paul Sartre, who was an essential author for many.

That launch was like a manifesto.
In another political collection called *Documentos*, the one most punished by the censors, we published *Los procesos de Moscú*, by the Trotskyite historian Pierre Broué, which took a critical view of Stalinism and the Moscow trials.

There was Enzensberger's view of Europe, a Marxist's view of poetry. Perhaps this wasn't exactly a provocation, but you evidently didn't publish to please the audience.
I believe that publishers have to be — and many of them are — diverse and authentic, and that their catalogues reflect their vision of the world to a great extent. There is a line by René Char, dedicated to the poets, that could also be applied to publishers: 'Develop your legitimate rarity.'

Has it been strange?
Anagrama had atypical characteristics when it began, especially in the 1970s, that tumultuous decade in which all the facets of the heterodox Left were present at Anagrama, but at the same time the Counterculture, the search for new currents of thought, many in France and not well known here, such as structuralism, anti-psychiatry, Freudo-Marxism... At the time I felt that the essay reflected more vitally the interests of that period and those of certain readers unsatisfied with Francoism. On the other hand, the novel, which had been and continues to be my great passion as a reader, excited me less and, furthermore,

it was an area occupied by publishers with much more pedigree and financial capacity, such as Seix Barral (subsequently Barral), Lumen, who was then just starting out, amongst others. Spain has produced many great publishers who I am often pleased to refer to. Focusing on the post-war period, I think that Janés was the first great Spanish publisher. A publisher in whom you could see, I think, one of the fundamental characteristics of those publishers who live their trade with a passion that we could call 'the emotion of craftsmanship.' To take care entirely of this passionate process of transforming a manuscript into a book. And if it's a translation, it would be advisable to look for the best translators, because a poor translation of a literary book is a crime, as it invalidates it for decades; to design the best possible covers, very often consulting with the authors – and the back covers, the book bands... All of this publishing process, until one arrives at the promotional aspect. As a journalist, you know how we at Anagrama are involved in non-stop promotion, an extensive information stream about new publications, continuous press conferences, lots of invitations to foreign writers... These are the weapons which permit us, as an independent publishing house, to compete with more powerful groups.

Your weapons have been taste and promotion, that non-stop promotion that you yourself have participated in, creating a following. Young publishers would like to be the Herralde of their generation.
I suppose that if this happens, there are also opposite feelings, as is normal and logical. Which is to say, perhaps that is what occurs – along with the obvious desire to 'kill the father'.

What I mean to say is, did you discover that style as you progressed or was it clear to you that this was the way to go?
It's been clear since the beginning, as one can see in the catalogue, but I learned along the way. I came from a family with no publishing

experience and I invented myself as a publisher, like so many others. But I did so by also taking advantage, not only of the model, but of the stimulus of these publishers I've mentioned, as well as of foreign publishers such as Einaudi, Feltrinelli, Gallimard, Minuit, Christian Bourgois and so many others.

Now, with your own experience and having observed others, what for you is the definition of a publisher?
I've already given you several, but for example, one could be: someone who creates a trustworthy backlist so that good readers can learn to trust unknown authors, one who supports those unknown authors, one who puts into practice the right approach with the writers one most believes in, thus helping them achieve the necessary tranquillity on which to build their careers. In short, the brand as a symbol. Christian Bourgois, for example, often used the expression *un passeur* when referring to a publisher's work, like a ferryman who transports a text from the river bank of literature, which is the author, to the bank of reading, which is the bookshop. A go-between.

In the midst of the maelstrom we are witnessing, what is the role of the publisher, what role awaits him?
We are living in times that are complicated and changeable for everyone, and any prediction is particularly risky. We are encountering two phenomena unknown to us before – there is a paradigm shift, so to speak. A global economic crisis of enormous proportions, further exacerbated in Spain by that damned real estate bubble; and then the e-book. It looks like the e-book will be more relevant in the mid-term, but it is here and, even though it has started out slowly, it is here to stay, which is going to change the relationship between publishers, authors, agents and booksellers. I am very much aware of bookshops, because since my adolescence, way before I became a publisher, I would spend hours in them, especially in a famous bookshop of that

time, Áncora y Delfín. It was run by Enric Folch, who later became a publisher, but who before was a great bookseller who would give you advice and take you to the back of the store, where the banned books were kept which entered by clandestine means. That role of the bookshop as a meeting point where readers can comment on what they are reading, where books are recommended, where reading clubs gather. Bookshops make cities. And this is very important.

With regards to culture, I am very much in favour of France – its *exception culturelle* – and the Lang Law on fixed prices: up until now, it has been like a barrier against the trivialisation that has invaded the cultural world, and is responsible in great part for the survival of bookshops. As you know, there was an attempt here in Spain during the first term of Aznar's ultra-neoliberal government to eliminate the fixed price law, but in Madrid and Barcelona the whole industry, including publishers, booksellers, authors and distributors, unanimously protested and caused an uproar, opting not to continue. We have the luck, and they the misfortune, of seeing the English and American models, where because of free pricing, the network of independent bookshops has been forced out of business.

To continue with this: there is an acute awareness of the importance of bookshops in France, and in June 2011 there was a large meeting in Lyon of more than 500 booksellers to discuss this subject in depth. One of the slogans was: 'My bookseller doesn't sell books by weight, he gives weight to books.' And how is this achieved? By knowing them all, by the way they are displayed, by being aware of which clients are interested in a certain book... In a sense, the booksellers, just by the way they choose books and how they display them in bookshops, also fulfil the role of prescription in much the same way as the publisher.

Does your concern with bookshops have to do with the fact that the e-book might cause them to disappear?
Today, there is a much more immediate factor: the crisis. The danger

lies in the economic crisis; we are observing that many bookshops are having difficulties; survival is not certain and they have difficulties with financing, which is why many books are returned, this is one of the most significant aspects of the past two years. Books that have little turnover, but contribute to the depth and diversity of a bookshop, once the pride of these same bookshops, simply can't be kept on the shelves the way they used to be. Quantitatively speaking, the e-book represents, for the time being, a very small part of the book market in Spain, France, or Italy. In the USA, its presence is more significant, but not much more, according to cultural press reports, because it has indeed gained a significant market share in the last few years. But if we were to discount encyclopaedias, legal and medical books, and things that are directly published in the e-book format, I would say its penetration is still minimal with respect to novels. And it has been a slow process.

In 2000 I attended the International Publisher's Conference in Buenos Aires, where some of the speakers expressed the belief that the e-book would make the physical book disappear in a few months or years. It was like 'The Terror Conference', because paper books already seemed obsolete in this hectic world. It was a false alarm.

Recently, Jünger Boss, the director of the Frankfurt Book Fair, reported the results of an international survey with more than 1,000 participants, and the final conclusion was that 40 per cent of those 1,000 thought that in 2018 e-book sales would exceed physical book sales for the first time. We are facing an equation with many unknown elements.

Then we also have the subject of illegal downloads. Literature and publishing have prospered thanks to copyright laws. That is why creators no longer depend on feudal lords or the Church, but on the market, with their works being protected by copyright regulation. Imaginative solutions, which I still don't know of, have to be found with respect to this.

In Spain, a little, great miracle has been performed with the three main publishing groups, coming to an agreement with respect to the e-book, and they have invited a whole group of independent publishers to participate, which Anagrama has done since the beginning. And in order to protect the network of booksellers, sales are to be made exclusively through bookshops. These are good intentions. For the time being, sales are slow, and once again it's difficult to make predictions. What has indeed increased a lot is the sale of various types of reading devices. On the other hand, the number of downloads – at least, of legal downloads – remains low. There is a curious asymmetry between the rise in the number of reading gadgets and the weaker increase in downloads.

At the moment we are currently living, will the brand continue to have such importance?
This could be one of the big problems with the digital book. The brand practically disappears, and in any event, the brand consists of those authors with many readers who have themselves become a brand. But for novice writers, being published and backed by a trustworthy publisher is extremely important. Later, when they become successful, that link, as you well know, weakens; as is quite logical. Now, according to my experience with Libranda [a Spanish platform for e-book distribution and diffusion], the ranking of bestsellers is practically symmetrical with that of the paper book. In our case, for example, Paul Auster and Ian McEwan are by far the highest sellers. But bookshops don't have the capacity to hold this enormous overproduction to which they are subject, and there are whimsical readers who search for unobtainable books. In this sense the e-book will have very valuable implications. For example, the e-book will reduce prices in Latin America, where books are more expensive due to shipping expenses, VAT in certain countries, exchange rates, etc. It will also enable the distribution of out of print books. In short,

there could be many advantages, but a delicate and complex balance must be sought out so that the invention doesn't get broken.

From your long experience, what disadvantages do you see in the e-book with regards to the aesthetic qualities of the traditional book the way we know it?
My experience comes from before the e-book and doesn't coincide.

But it coincides in time.
It's an encounter and I hope it won't be a collision. Like so many readers – like almost all of us I would say, except the very youngest generation – I am addicted to the book as an object, to its well-crafted composition, to the paper, to all those veritable clichés that have been said. I am addicted to the traditional book. I think it was Umberto Eco who said: 'The hammer, the wheel, the scissors or the book are perfect objects.' One can add a few rococo ornaments, but that's it, the book is a perfect object. Especially when it is made with the 'emotion of craftsmanship' which I mentioned at the beginning of the interview.

In 1995 or 1996, when new technologies began to appear, it was said at the Frankfurt Book Fair that the book, this perfect object, would dissappear, and yet, here it is still.
Yes indeed, and it's published very well. In the bookshop sector we have seen the phenomenon of two large chains like Borders, going bankrupt, and Barnes and Noble, up for sale. During the last few years independent bookshops have practically disappeared, although there is now a revival. Robert McCrum, an excellent journalist and former publisher, said: 'Today we are seeing important spending cutbacks in or the actual disappearance of public libraries and they have been an English institution more solid than the Queen of England.' That is true, but from an optimistic point of view there is also

the compensatory phenomenon of the emergence in England of ever more reading clubs, which are here in their infancy, where the passion for reading is transmitted; and a certain revival of independent bookshops after many years of their having practically disappeared.

Will the publisher become someone different? Will the Herralde of the e-book era maintain the same parameters? You say you can't be a prophet, but a publisher is always a prophet: you publish a book and you believe it's going to work out.
Like everything else, the spirit of the times will affect the publisher and he will have to intervene more frequently in technological matters, be more involved in phenomena such as blogs... There are a couple of young people here at the company attending to those blogs that seem to be more in tune with our publishing house; we also have a web page, we are on Facebook, Twitter, etc.

How do you feel in this universe, which is affecting your vocation in such an important way?
A bit perplexed as I face the future. Nevertheless, at the moment it is still possible to apply the basic principles of publishing as I understand it, whilst also increasing one's curiosity with regards to new technology. Coming back to the crisis, it has caused publishing to become more and more mimetic. This tendency has always existed, but today Stieg Larsson comes out and 50 possible Larssons appear; a successful historical novel appears and you have a historical novel boom; crime fiction... I've been a great reader of detective or crime fiction myself and I published Patricia Highsmith, but in Spain it sold rather slowly. And suddenly, now there's an explosion of interest.
Out of an understandable need to survive, there are many publishers who are more mimetic and less individual than others. Einaudi has an expression that refers to the 'yes' publisher and the 'no' publisher, which goes something like this: 'the "yes" publisher is the one who

is fundamentally concerned with good literature, with profound and lucid essays, and who wants each book to be valuable and original in its own right; versus the "no" publisher, who repeats past formulas and simply goes in serch of the possible bestseller as a sequel to previous experiences.' The 'yes' publisher is the one who is devoted to the quest for that which enriches the reader. When I was starting out, one of the most gratifying experiences was the creation of *Distribuciones de Enlace*, in which eight independent publishers made an alliance for the first time, sharing a common distribution network and a common paperback collection. Carlos Barral, Pedro Altares, Beatriz de Moura, Esther Tusquets, and Alfonso Carlos Comín... all participated. Our intention was to help change the social and cultural future of Spain—perhaps in an insufficient measure—through publishing, in the face of Franco's imminent death. At least we fought with all our passion. And we had a lot of fun, something which is very important and I would say necessary for the process.

You mention what Einaudi used to say about the 'yes' publisher and the 'no' publisher, and previously you mentioned the bestsellers lists. It appears that the reader favours the 'no' publisher.
I'm afraid that is so.

In your opinion, what are the consequences of this for publishing houses such as yours?
Good literature in general has always been a minority or comparatively minority sector. For example, the publisher and star backlist of the 1960s, Biblioteca Breve, at Carlos Barral's Seix Barral, published books that with luck sold only a few thousand copies. At the time, the 'Market', with capital letters, did not exist as such, writers didn't talk about advances or money, simply because there wasn't any, there was a total lack of it in this sense. In other words, it has always been mainly a minority sector. In any event, the Spain of the 1980s, with

economic development, more access to universities and a lot of well-known factors, also witnessed a systematic growth in successful sales of so-called quality literature, which still persists today, but to a lesser degree, because it has also been punished.

There has been a traditional relationship, solid or not depending on the case, between publisher and author. Nowadays, new technology allows authors to have control over their own work, when previously it was the publisher who had control, the person who published it. How do you see this relationship? What was the relationship with the author like, and how do you imagine it might be?
The relationship with the author has gone through quite a few stages, beginning with the feudal stage. Even in the 20th century, in France, when they published an author for the first time, they had the so-called *droit de suite* clause, by which the publisher had the rights for the next five books. In other words, they practically became the possession of the publisher. This has lessened over the decades. Now we are at the extreme opposite, owing to the appearance of literary agents and large publishing houses. Naturally, faced with the necessity for turnover, advances grew exponentially, very often above realistic sales estimates, which has contributed to a contraction of the relationship between the author and the publisher. And a few agents have specialised in this, because if these relationships are reduced, the transition to another brand is less painful and troubled.
With respect to the e-book, I would also say it is too early to know, because sales are still too small and percentages are still being discussed; there have already been several initiatives, although very embryonic, by agents who want to become publishers. Andrew Wylie, was the first with Odyssey, but Random House, who published his authors, stepped in and told him that if he continued along that line they would no longer sign any contracts with him. And he has desisted. For the time being. A short time after, the literary agent

Ed Victor announced his intention to start publishing books, to be the publisher of six books which were out of print; in the following year, he would come out with another six, and would not abandon the idea of publishing unpublished texts. In a sense he took up his old vocation as publisher again, because when I met him he was the second-in-command at Jonathan Cape, the most prestigious publisher in Britain. The publishing bug is powerful. Carmen Balcells used to say: 'The thing about publishing is that it's very sexy, and being the publisher is the sexiest thing of all.'

Do you also believe that?
No, more than sexy, it's very attractive while one is able to practise it. This is evident in a subject we haven't discussed, not only in Spain, but also all over the world: the great number of small, very literary publishers who are condemned, so to speak, to excellence. In order to create an identity and have a fan club in the midst of this avalanche of books, they have to be excellent and imaginative, without a break. And no small number of them are just that.

Before, you talked about the agents who strive to become publishers. You know that when something happens only once, despite the one who initiates it having possible regrets later on, it tends to end up happening again.
It is something that's latent. It's an additional problem.

And what is your attitude? Because Random House threatened and followed through with their threat, you as a publisher...
But that is something an effective power such as Planeta, Random or Santillana can do, but not an independent publishing house here in Spain.

In other words, publishers should consider themselves defeated.
Not necessarily. If you enter like an bull in a china shop, and publish

1,000 books a year, this does cause a deep trauma, but for the time being, Andrew Wylie and Ed Victor's initiatives have been experiments.
And we return to the difficulty of making predictions: depending on
how things go for them with these experiments, they will increase
them or maintain them at a stable level or simply abandon them.

**Maybe it's that you have made this trade so sexy that the agents see
that it might have its appeal.**
Ask Carmen Balcells about this, she has the copyright. I was just
quoting her phrase.

**Throughout the years, you've seen how agents have been acquiring
dominance and capital importance: how have you seen this influen-
cing your work or that of other publishers, and the work of the
authors? How has this affected the relationship between publisher
and author?**
As always, it depends on each of the authors, each of the agents and
each of the publishers. I have very good relationships with many
literary agents—with most of them; as well as with most authors.
In order to make the transition from one publisher to another and to
participate in this whole system of literary prizes that are irrigating
the country, I think an agent is more useful. With respect to international dissemination, there are some agents who have done a very
good job: Carmen Balcells, or more recently, Antonia Kerrigan. But
publishers have also done this for many years—for example, Anagrama. A literary publisher is more effective than an agent when
it comes to promoting good but little-known literary writers. This
is an important aspect that has been proven. Why? Because there is
a kind of informal club of publishers in different countries and we
share the same wavelength and we know each other's tastes, we're
publishers who publish basically for the pleasure of publishing good
books. Naturally, we try to keep this pleasure alive, so that it doesn't

become a tragedy and the publishing house disappears. There is a basic principle: the publishing of minority – or still minority – authors, for the pleasure of good literature. That said, to negotiate the macro-rights of a García Márquez or a Vargas Llosa, a literary agent is infinitely better.

Let's get back to the author. You have seen many authors making their careers, but do you find that the author today, especially the young author, has the same attitude as when they used to come to see you? In a world where there are agents and rights they can control, do young authors have the same attitude towards their first book, or has it already changed?
In general, when an author writes his first book, things have not changed. A few books later is when some literary agent says: 'Well now, let's have a look at this one here who is budding... Let's try tempting him.'

They hover around.
Waiting for the moment to sign him up. Continuing without an agent also depends on the efficiency of the publisher and on the author's perception of the work being done – not only how publishing is done in Spain and Latin America, which is another very important subject, but also regarding translations and international dissemination. As an example, with Alejandro Zambra, a young author of three unique, excellent short novels, we have already signed ten contracts for *Bonsái* and six for *La vida privada de los árboles*, but with the last novel, *Formas de volver a casa*, before publishing it, we sent a PDF document to various publishing houses, and five have bought it, amongst them Farrar, Straus and Giroux. Natasha Wimmer, Bolaño's translator, recommended him, saying: 'The only author I've recommended in these years is Zambra.' And the others are Mondadori, Suhrkamp, Éditions de l'Olivier and Karaat. And besides the international dissemination

of Zambra, from Anagrama we have launched Roberto Bolaño, Álvaro Pombo, Javier Marías, Rafael Chirbes, Enrique Vila-Matas... minority authors a priori, but who soon had a nucleus of very attentive publishers of which I would like to mention three: Christian Bourgois, who died recently, was the one with whom I dealt most directly. He was a great publisher and a great friend, who published in France many of the best authors in the Spanish language of the last decades. And Christopher MacLehose of Harvill in the United Kingdom. The third would be Siegfried Unseld, the publisher of Suhrkamp.

Unseld was capable of walking half way around the world to buy an author a sandwich. That is one of the characteristics of the publisher, the man who is proud of someone else's success. It is a very interesting publisher's characteristic. Do you think that continues to be so, that enthusiasm for the other to succeed?
In my case, that of Zambra has filled me with an immense satisfaction. Another recent case worth mentioning is that of Juan Pablo Villalobos, a young Mexican author living in Barcelona, unknown in Mexico and Spain, and whose first novel, *Down the Rabbit Hole*, about drug trafficking seen through the eyes of a small child, was translated into eight or nine languages. It is very gratifying to see how the enthusiasm we have invested in totally unknown authors is widely applauded and celebrated by the majority of publishers we value. It's a very interesting case, that of Villalobos. I sent it to Berenberg, who was Wagenbach's Spanish literary consultant and later Antje Kunstmann's literary consultant. He began an exquisite non-fiction publishing house a few years ago. I sent him *Down the Rabbit Hole* and he liked it so much that he decided to start a fiction series with this book.

In other words, you remain enthusiastic and continue the non-stop promotion of your books.
These are the issues that most interest me, choosing and actively

participating in the production of the book, and afterwards in its promotion. Naturally there are very capable professionals in the press department, the editing department, etc., but I intervene very assiduously. Another characteristic of the publishing house, as you know, especially in the last ten years, is a more and more persistent focus on Latin America, with a larger number of Latin American authors being published. I think they make up about half of the authors published in the Spanish language. And also the systematic publishing of their books in their native countries and in Spain, Argentina and Mexico, and to a lesser degree in Chile, Venezuela, Peru... This has contributed very positively to the dissemination of Anagrama in Latin America. It has always been good, but this has reinforced it.

You have taken risks. Perhaps what is happening now is that young authors can't publish unless an established publisher takes the risk. But if things continue as they have been, if the young don't publish the young...
Comparisons between different periods of time are also difficult because now, in order to take risks, one must take into account real possibilities. Many of these publishing houses start out with one or two people publishing ten or 15 books a year. Anagrama also started out with two people, a secretary and myself, but published too much from the first year on. Now times are difficult, the crisis is hitting everybody and it is also affecting the bookshops. Although the more dedicated bookshops act like incubators for these new brands and give them preferential treatment. This can be seen in some of the best bookshops in Spain. With respect to taking risks: there are many publishers with few economic resources, but since, as one might put it, the global stock of good books that haven't been translated, or are of more minority interest, or were in a publisher's catalogue whose rights have expired is immense, they have got the impression that republishing them would be profitable and have reissued them.

But there are also many among them who are imaginative, who are creating a personal profile in exploring little known territories, as is the case with Minúscula, Acantilado before them, and others like Libros del Asteroide, Global Rhythm, Alpha Decay, Errata Naturae, Periférica... There are many others I haven't mentioned, but there are quite a few to whom one could apply the old saying, 'to choose is to exclude'; one can see who is publisher material, though possessing as well both the tenacity and luck necessary to continue is a different thing.

What is definitely true is that we are talking about the publishing crisis, the bookshop crisis, the book crisis – and all the time, more imprints are appearing. You've mentioned almost eight or nine new publishers; does that mean that they are crazy, or is this the future?
They are a little bit crazy, as all of us are, starting with publishers. This profession has some components which are a bit mad. I would say that up until about ten years ago, it seemed like the territory was already occupied by the three main groups, a few veteran publishing houses, and not much else. But precisely ten years ago, I wrote an article, 'The New Disobedients', in which I talked about some 20 new publishing houses that had just appeared, although today, instead of an article I would have to write a book, because there would be about 200 or 300 of them! How does one explain this? Thanks to new technology, costs have come down significantly, smaller print runs can be done and books can have a reasonable sales price, because previously, small print runs would cause expenses to skyrocket. You can also look for books without advances or with small advances, sometimes with old translations – in other words: it is possible to take intelligent advantage of the state of affairs. And to have a wartime economy with just one or two people working, that is to say, 'exploitation and self-exploitation'. It's also important to persist in order to create the trademark, to build credibility. And lastly, some

connect very well with their contemporaries, with young people in their twenties and thirties, through an active presence conducive to online encounters.

A third phase. What makes this such a crazy trade?
The fact that this is an absolutely unpredictable business. Since the success of a book depends on so many factors, every book is a gamble. I remember that when I began to publish, my father, who was a metal manufacturer, would ask me how things were going, and thought it was crazy that I would risk sending books to Latin America without insurance or anything. And not to mention the Francoist censorship and book confiscations.
And many other factors. I think it is lived with more intensity due to the relationship with the authors, in that each product is a prototype, especially the literary books; bestsellers and their endless sequels are another story. The relationship with the press, which is both friendly and complicated, or the backlist which has to be defended in the face of multiple attacks from the other publishers. In other words, it requires passion, a dedication and a discipline that really turn it into something mad and passionate.

You began with an enthusiasm that you've described in many articles; it is apparent in everything you do. There was the agreement you made with Feltrinelli, and for those of us who had educated ourselves with books from Anagrama it was a bit traumatic at first, but later on everyone accepted it as something natural, as something that had to be done. How did you take it?
Not even publishers are immortal; consequently we had to think of a solution for the company's future, always a 'future' in inverted commas, because everything is provisional, as we know only too well. Pretending to be a sensible person, I said to myself: what is the best solution? Naturally I thought we could opt for one of the big Spanish

or foreign groups that had been interested in Anagrama; I had always told them that I felt very flattered, and that when the time came, I would think about it.

And I had no doubts. Conditions for a merger of independent publishers in Spain were not the right ones. With respect to foreign publishing houses, Feltrinelli was by far my favourite, first, because of my friendship with Inge, and later with Carlo, as well as for being in tune with the Feltrinelli project. For his part, Carlo had told me for years: 'If you are ever interested in selling Anagrama, or part of it, I would be thrilled.' We came to an agreement very quickly; neither of us had any problem.

How do you feel now when you sit alongside a partner?
We sat down as partners one day, the day we signed the definitive contract for everything we had agreed on and provisionally signed. But I feel totally in tune with Carlo. And there is a fruitful exchange of information. He comes to Anagrama as someone who likes it.

And you come to Feltrinelli as someone who likes Feltrinelli.
Exactly.

What interests you about Feltrinelli?
The fact that it's a family business with enormous power, that it's fundamentally based on the book, through its publishing arm and the 104 Feltrinelli bookshops.

It's a family business based on the book.
On the love for the book. And also on the desire to help change society, to improve it; this is quite unequivocal. They are now aware of the fact that the world is changing and, as one of their executives said in a recent interview, there seems to be a tendency towards multi-product establishments: they sell books, DVD, all kinds of technological

gadgets in order to be able – precisely thanks to this – to continue selling books.

Feltrinelli represents a certain type of publishing in Europe, as do Anagrama and others. Is there something that distinguishes European publishing from, for example, that most fabulous of competitors, the United States?
I would say that the European publishing world is more solid and more literary. In the American publishing world, there are some publishers, such as Knopf or Farrar, Straus and Giroux, that are part of larger groups, but maintain their literary independence; however, many have disappeared or are not very important. The famous City Lights Books is very important historically and qualitatively speaking, but not quantitatively. Then there are many serious and solvent university publishing houses, but the wave of mercantilism is also affecting them considerably. And there is another big subject, the subject of translations. There has been the tremendous success of Bolaño, the García Márquez phenomenon many years ago... But very few English translations are being published in England or the United States. There is an excellent book, *The World Republic of Letters* by Pascale Casanova, whose thesis is that, although France or French literature have not shone in a spectacular way for years, Paris continues to be the hub necessary for the international dissemination of authors, because much more is translated there and much sooner than in the big groups of New York and London.

PERSONAL LIBRARY

1. Kafka, Franz. *The Essential Kafka Boxed Set*,
Penguin Books, London, 2004
2. Borges, Jorge Luis. *Collected Fictions*,
Penguin Books, London, 1999
3. Proust, Marcel. *In Search of Lost Time*, Modern
Library, New York, 2003
4. Faulkner, William. *As I Lay Dying*, W.W. Norton,
New York, 2010
5. Scott Fitzgerald, F. *The Great Gatsby*, Penguin
Books, New York, 2011
6. Nabokov, Vladimir. *Lolita*, Penguin Classics,
London, 2012
7. Gombrowicz, Witold. *Ferdydurke*, Yale University
Press, New Haven, USA, 2012
8. Martín Santos, Luis. *Time of Silence*, Columbia
University Press, New York, 1989
9. The poetry of Jaime Gil de Biedma
10. Bolaño, Roberto. *2666*, Picador, London, 2009

SIGRID KRAUS

Editorial Director of Ediciones Salamandra

IN SPAIN THE BOOKSELLER SUFFERS FROM
A GREAT LONELINESS

In the atmosphere that surrounds Sigrid Kraus in Salamandra, the Spanish publishing house she directs and which publishes *Harry Potter*, it would be possible to record a classical music concert in high fidelity. In the next room, in silence, Pedro del Carril, her husband, who is in charge of the financial side of the business, works with numbers. Pedro comes from a very long line of traditional publishers, and Sigrid became a publisher due to her passion for reading. That is the substance of her work. And as in every other place where people read, here the silence feels like a house rule followed to the letter. Their company has just celebrated its first ten years, in the course of which J.K. Rowling's series has brought them a now legendary success (and substantial livelihood), and thanks mainly to those books, conceived and written for children or adolescents, they have built a genuinely adult publishing house, courageously, with their eyes open to what is being written beyond the frontiers of the Spanish language. Indeed, until now they have never published any work originally written in Spanish.

We break the silence where they work, so that Sigrid, a 47-year-old German, can tell us what lies behind the story and give us her insight into today's uncertainties. At one point, she catches our attention: 'In Spain, booksellers suffer from a great loneliness.' We spoke before of how a publishing house can be built that transcends the very utopian objectives that its seemingly deluded founders once contemplated.

How did you do it?
We began as Emecé, where Pedro del Carril had been working. Behind Emecé, there was a very long history in Argentina, and Pedro was their representative in Spain. At the time, that publishing house was the Gallimard of Latin America. As for myself, I have breathed books ever since I was a child. This was because my grandfather was an author, and such things make a difference.

What is this you say about breathing books?
Everything that is around you. Pedro had to go and count books during the holidays from the age of 15, and he spent his summer holidays with Adolfo Bioy Casares, he was with Jorge Luis Borges at home drinking tea; and in my own home, my grandfather was writing non-fiction books and talking, having lunch and quarrelling with his publisher. That is what I mean by breathing books. Both of us grew up in this kind of environment.

From Emecé you brought with you the smell of books. And the experience of editing.
I was educated in Germany, as an editor and as a bookseller... There it is wonderful: you work in a publishing house, you are paid a salary, you spend three months in each department over a period of two-and-a-half years and at the same time you go to a kind of university specialising only in the world of publishing... Later you are sent to work in printing houses, in bookshops... Nothing could be better. I had done extensive internships with publishers of the Bertelsmann group in London, in order to get to know the group from the inside.

I worked with a literary agent and then went to Círculo de Lectores, but that didn't last long. By then Pedro was already here starting up Emecé with very few resources, practically on his own, in a dim room. Every day I would tell him the problems I was having with this or that book, until finally he said: 'If we are going to talk about that, I think I would prefer that you tell me about our own books. Come and work with me.' And that led to Salamandra, ten years ago.

A couple work together in a dim room and build up a publishing house... What do you have to do to break the silence that is there when something is being born?
Total and absolute belief in your books. I remember that at our first working lunch with our distributor, he was looking elsewhere during the meal. We were explaining the book to him and he was looking out of the window, enjoying the food and drinking the wine. I was saying to myself: 'This man is not even listening to me! How are we going to do it?' I think there is an advantage in being young and ignorant at the same time, because you believe everything is possible, that you can obtain anything. Now it would be impossible for me to do it. It was a very difficult moment in Spain, the moment of the big crash... But there was something good too: we were born into opposition, to fight against something, like a son who confronts his father. We wanted to do something different, to show that the result of our energy would work. Attempting such a thing is in itself a privilege.

Pedro de Carril broke with tradition. In times of catastrophe, doesn't that produce an enormous sense of the abyss? When one breaks with one's father, what is broken?
I think that Pedro was looking for this void. When you have grown up in a family framework, with a name that is well-known, what you want is to just be Pedro. The same happened to me: I loved books,

I wanted to work with books and the rest was all the same to me. Since the age of 15, I've only ever wanted to make books. Wherever.

What did you believe in so firmly?
I believed that if you made a good book, a well-written book, attractive, and with a beautiful cover, then it would be a book that would work well.

And you realised that it was not so easy. How was that?
There is a long chain of people between you and the reader, and you have to convince these people that your book is better, more worthy than the thousands of other books that are just as good, just as nice and well edited as yours. Convincing this chain of people has been our work for years and years. A slow process, in which you have to win them over one by one, convince the bookseller, make friends with the distributors, ask them for a chance... We did something unusual very early on: we hired a salesperson of our own, a woman, who would take only our books from bookshop to bookshop. At that time nobody was doing it.

What was your objective?
People said to us: 'You have to create a niche, because it's that niche that is going to survive!'

What a horrible word, 'niche'.
We used to say to them: 'No way! We are going to be loyal to our intuition.' We have always believed that honesty will take us far: honesty with the bookseller, with the reader, with the journalist, with the distributor and with the writer. That is fundamental in our business. It is something that is not very common and a lot of mistakes come from that. You have to be firmly convinced of what you are doing, and you don't have to lie, you don't have to cheat. That

was one of our objectives. The other one was to follow intuition, our intuition. If a book for children appeared that I liked, then we would publish it. If I like the novel of a dead Hungarian, we publish it too... The intuition, the instinct.

Nowadays books look like they carry the same old stamp. How was it, that quest?
Now what people do is go backwards. So Stieg Larsson is a winner? Everybody searches for another Stieg Larsson. *Harry Potter* is a winner? Everybody searches for another *Harry Potter*. Why? Because many of them work in big corporations, and a man in a big corporation doesn't understand it when you say to him: 'Now look here, no, we are going to take a risk and we are going to gamble blindly on this book or this author, even if nobody knows whether it is going to work or not.' My fellow professionals, who are very good editors too, have to convince their superiors with arguments like: 'No, this is OK. It's like Stieg Larsson, or like Stephenie Meyer...' They need to argue in this way to impose a book. I don't need to. That is my privilege.

This necessity for repeating the formulas, doesn't it convert book-shops into very flat planes where everything seems to be C, where there is no A or B?
Yes. And the worst thing is that what I receive from abroad is the same. More and more, everything is becoming more uniform. I think that even some writers are already conforming to these pressures. Their agents must be saying to them that they must try to do something like Stephenie Meyer or someone else, because that is what people want. It is a big mistake!

Is that the real crisis of the book?
Yes. For years I have been saying that the real crisis of the book will

have its origin in its creation, and not in the final product. We have become so obsessed with the end product of the book, how it will be, whether it will be electronic or not, how we are going to distribute it... When what should be preoccupying us is the process of its creation, that an author should sit down and write what he has to write, what comes from within him... And that is becoming more difficult all the time.

Inge Feltrinelli, whose publishing house has also inherited a tradition of intuition, was telling us that what is happening is a general levelling down, in bookshops as well as in minds, even in conversation. Everything has to be the same as it is already. What feeling do you have about all this?
It is one of the dangers of the globalised world. Even if the globalised world sounds nice and has many advantages, at the same time it is a standardisation of the world. The Internet too makes us all become more and more similar, more and more the same. Who are the interesting writers emerging now? The other day I read the word 'nerd', which in the 1980s was derogatory; now it is the one who is strange, the one who deliberates, the one who is crazy or creative, the strange guy who, when he was a child, was playing alone in the playground... They are the ones, the few, who are giving us the ideas now. They are the ones from Apple, Google... The rare ones, that our educational system is crushing completely. And a writer is a nerd too. And he is also being crushed.

One can see now how writers are worrying about following the trends, about contracts, about the relationship with their agents... Perhaps the artistic habit is missing.
We are guilty too. We have entangled them, we have placed them inside this net. The author who has had success is under so much pressure from the industry to sell what he has not yet written... For

example, you make contracts for several books, and the writers are caught in these contracts because they have to write the books...

What can be done to make the book recover its place in society?
The time that is coming now, which is going to be tough because they say the electronic book will conquer, I don't for one minute believe it will be uniform, I think all books will coexist together. It might happen that the paper book will be left in a corner, that it will be found in less important places, that it will lose all the glamour it has; but it could also happen, that things will calm down and the book will return to the same place it occupied before.

And that there will be fewer books published?
They will also have to publish far fewer books. Maybe due to this revolution less will be published. I met this big publishing magnate who said to me: 'I think the big publishing houses like ours will not be able to exist in the future, they will have to break down into small entities of service-providing units, they will have to work here and there...' Maybe that would not be so bad and we will return to a more human scale, in accordance with what the author is.

With respect to these prophesied catastrophes, what is your intuition?
I think that electronic books and paper books are going to coexist for many years more. We can still continue publishing calmly for a long time yet. There will always be someone reading paper books. I myself have been reading electronic books for three years now and I haven't found them, let's say, very sexy. And I'm worried about the matter of copyright, it remains unclear.

What problem do you see?
There is this whole tendency on the Net to say that a book can be downloaded without paying. There are some people with a very idealistic

notion of the world, where everything is shared with everybody and you don't have to pay for the intangible. If that is how things are, we shouldn't have to pay for the tangible either. Should it be so only for books but not for cars? How can they say this? Their ideals are very respectable – they are not monsters, poor things – but I see a danger here, and it is that we have failed in their education. We have educated generations who have not understood the concept and the wonder of copyright, they do not realise that huge progress has been made since the Renaissance, when the artist was finally saved from patronage. Now, if this continues, the artist will have to go back to the patron.

And what is the position of Salamandra with respect to the e-book?
We are doing everything very slowly; the privilege of being independent, small or medium, is that you can observe how the big firms go about it. And see what happens.

Are you nervous about it?
No, not at all. Honestly, at the moment I'm not too nervous about it. I find it strange to think that the wonderful thing about my work is that in the end there is an object. When I read an original work, I tend to visualise a book in my mind, and that vision is what I try to transmit... To think that this final product is a text on a screen would mean that my work doesn't exist anymore. Then there is no longer an object, there's no longer an artisan. And I consider myself an artisan. If there were no object, it would be an entirely different thing...

What would this publisher without an object be?
We are going to be publicists and not artisans. We will be worrying about how to succeed in making the book stand out on the Internet or wherever. That is advertising. It is not producing a beautiful object that attracts someone.

Are there any problems specific to Spain with regards to the health of the book?
The only criticism that I can make about Spain, a country I adore, is how education is neglected; throughout all historical periods. And that is a problem for the bookshop too. The bookseller is engulfed by an enormous loneliness. He has had to teach himself, learning as he goes. He ought to have more training, more help, courses where he can go to learn, to form himself, prepare himself... There, on the bookshop, is where attention should now be focused.

PERSONAL LIBRARY

1. Mitchell, Margaret. *Gone with the Wind*, Scribner, New York, 2011
2. Zweig, Stefan. *The World of Yesterday*, Pushkin Press, London, 2010
3. Pessoa, Fernando. *Message*, Shearsman Books, Bristol, UK, 2007
4. Machado de Assis, Joaquim Maria. *Don Casmurro*, Farrar, Straus and Giroux, New York, 2009
5. Von Kügelgen, Wilhelm. *Bygone Days: Or, an Old Man's Reminiscences of his Youth*, Nabu Press, USA, 2010
6. García Márquez, Gabriel. *One Hundred Years of Solitude*, Harper Perennial Modern Classics, New York, 2006
7. Mendoza, Eduardo. *The City of Marvels*, Pocket Books, New York, 1990
8. Klemperer, Victor. *The Klemperer Diaries*, Orion Publishing, London, 2004
9. Seth, Vikram. *A Suitable Boy*, Orion Publishing, London, 2012
10. Smith, Zadie. *White Teeth*, Penguin Books, London, 2011

MICHAEL KRÜGER

Editorial Director of Hanser Verlag

EDITORS ARE NO LONGER PASSIONATE READERS

Michael Krüger (born 1943, German poet, novelist and editor) is the Editorial Director of Hanser, one of the great literary publishing houses of Europe. In front of the airy windows of his office in Munich are some magnificent trees, which he, as a poet of irony and memory, identifies with those who will be watching us in the future. What about the present? That's the key question today: what will happen to the book as we currently know it? What will happen, according to him as author and editor? In one of his books of poems he has some beautiful lines about memory: 'Sometimes childhood/sends me a postcard.' What does memory tell the author? What postcard does it send? He is one of that breed of literary editors that Europe produces, such as Carlos Barral, Roberto Calasso, Jaime Salinas, Beatriz de Moura, Jorge Herralde. He is also a poet and novelist. He is the editor of Franz Kafka and Elias Canetti. So he feels an enormous respect for the text as we have always known it, the same respect he feels for the passing of time. We wanted to talk to him about that, about the time that is approaching, about the challenges that the world created by his fellow countryman Gutenberg now faces.

You said in one of your books: 'To go on your way, as if death wasn't walking behind you.' Sometimes we live our lives as if death had nothing to do with us. And there they are, the books, just as we have always known them. Will these books die?

Really good books have a longer life than a man. And this is a bizarre situation. Like sitting in front of a blank piece of paper in the morning. But one fine day the author will die and his book will remain there. That's the fascinating thing about a book: it has its own life; its only relationship with the author is that it carries his name. The strange thing is that everyone – the stupid, the intelligent, the educated and the ignorant – can read a book in a different way. The text has its own life. The moment you publish a book, you should know that it will probably live much longer than you as an author. And the only person who will take care of it is the publisher. The publisher has the duty to keep the book alive even if its author is dead. After the author dies, the only ones who remain are the publisher and the text. The book is a living organism.

And there is the reader.

The book is always waiting for a reader. If the reader doesn't come, it dies. That's why publishers have the duty of keeping it alive. What does that mean? Everybody knows that 90 per cent of the books published in 2011 will not have survived a year later. Most of the books you see in a store have a shelf-life of six months; the other 10 per cent might have a longer life. Some books, even if they are important, are forgotten. But suddenly, someone comes along, picks it up and says: 'This is a work of art, we should read it again.' And often readers follow this advice. Kafka is a good example. While he was alive he published some 200 pages that were read by a thousand people. Just a thousand people! No one else. However, after the war, someone picked up the book and said: 'This book describes the state of the human condition during the First World War perfectly and it should be read again.' Now it is being read by people all over the world.

And, in his own time, he was virtually unpublished.
While he was alive nobody cared about what Kafka wrote. The editor's duty is to listen to the music of the times. This music is always searching for someone and a text can always be revitalised. For example, two years ago we published what I would call the most appropriate translation of *Don Quixote*. Of course, there were already many translations into German, about ten or 15. However, we thought that its allegories might be interesting for the public today, that they could find a new public. We thought it would be interesting to read it now in this capitalist, Europeanist historical moment, in which there are so many new battles with windmills. The interesting thing is that the new translation has had an enormous success. What we didn't expect was that the metaphorical and allegorical situation of Don Quixote and Sancho Panza fitted so perfectly with the current situation in the world. The editor should know that books, even if they are 500 years old, can have a new life. Imagine *Hamlet* today...

The human condition is always the same.
Correct. And it doesn't change at an accelerated rate. The period of life for a human being is very short; because it is so short, people should read the good books that already exist. And the editor should know what books – from the past and from the present – could really catch the attention of a disoriented reader. In the last few years, we have experienced so many changes in the way we see the world, our existence, politics, the European Union. People and their thinking have changed

so much. That's what politicians should have in mind: everything is different, and perhaps authors understand this better than anyone else. Every country has its authors. We should pay attention to what they write about – and so should the politicians. I believe that people's thoughts are only correctly described in literature. Up until the 1950s, people only had literature to understand different worlds. Nowadays, we have other ways of understanding how we are. But we should always use literature to really understand people's ways of thinking.

So you say your work consists in reviving dead books? Talking about modern books, how do you select them?
It's something that comes with experience. I think many editors today do not read. They are so concerned with reading contemporary books and reviews that they are no longer reading for pleasure. They aren't passionate readers. And 80 per cent or 90 per cent of the books they publish will disappear next year. Of course, we have to feed ourselves and our writers; the show must go on. But the show has nothing to do with the person sitting alone and writing. The job of writing: that's what fascinates me. That has never changed. The writer continues to sit in front of a blank sheet of paper. The writing process has nothing to do with new technology. It's just that the tools have improved for the writer, nothing else.

In one of your books, you say the future is a joke. Can we talk about the future as if it were a joke?
If you were my age of course you could talk about the future with a sense of humour. Nobody was able to predict the global crisis that we are suffering. Not even people with a high educational level, the wealthy, the educated. No one! Nobody thought there would be a reunification of Germany. Nobody thought that there would be an uprising in Africa. Nobody thought Facebook was going to change society. Twenty years ago, no one thought people would be walking

down the streets with a mobile phone in their hands. Before, I was happy just reading the paper in the morning. Today, some people are not satisfied if they don't receive 15 newspapers on their computers daily. But in the end, I will sit down and stare at the tree and house I have in front of me. And I will die with that tree in front of my eyes.

Many changes. How will they affect our reading habits?
They affect our very existence. Which means that at the moment, nobody has time. It is very common to hear someone saying: 'I don't have the time!' If you spend even a very brief moment reading rubbish you know you're missing out on reading a poem by Góngora. The more trash there is, the less time you will have for yourself. It is a paradoxical situation: hearing people complain that they do not have enough time. Because they do have it! And, of course, all these ups and downs affect reading. Because we can't read faster. Marcel Proust can't be read in less than three months. And that makes the machine angry. The machine wants a person to read Proust in two days. The machine will think of creating shorter formats, summaries, comic strips... This situation reminds me of a quote from Woody Allen: after reading Dostoyevsky he was asked about the book, and he answered: 'The only thing I can say about it is it's by a Russian.' Reading is totally opposite to this acceleration, to this rhythm. Any other thing can be adapted to this speed, but not reading.

Will these changes also affect the act of writing? And will they affect the publishing houses?
I've just got back from New York, where they told me that now 35 per cent of books are going to be available in e-book format. And this percentage could rise. E-books are cheaper, they do not need paper, the trees are happy. Also, it means you can store hundreds of books in your computer, you do not need physical space to keep them in. I believe all this is having an enormous impact on the publishing world.

Small bookshops are closing. Within the next five years I will have to reorganise our framework here. I will need more people to supervise electronic sales and to promote books through the social networks. And they will have to get into blogs. Today, writing is linked to introducing an idea into an electronic universe. Ideas are faster than books. When, back in 1858, someone found out about the mathematical solution to a problem, the news of that finding travelled slowly until it was approved and adopted. Now, you can share a mathematical solution with the whole world within eight minutes.

And will publishers continue to be the guardians of books?
For the next 20 years, publishers will continue to exist. Maybe there will not be as many as today, but many will survive. The market for the publishing industry is decreasing. Print runs are getting smaller and costs are getting higher. In ten or 20 years time, a book will be too expensive for a young reader. Instead of buying the book, they will just print out Shakespeare's Sonnets directly. And this takes us to the matter of the copyright. That is the big problem. Most of the books and information that are available in a bookshop can be found on the Internet. One can pay for the contents or one can commit piracy. If the will to buy books disappears, books will disappear. And that is what has happened in the publishing industry. I do not know how it will work out in Spain, but in Germany authors go on book tours and give talks. If they can give 14 talks in a year, they reach the public and can make the necessary amount of money to live on, apart from what they can get from the actual sales.

They are troubadours.
And in their role as troubadours, authors can sell their books in that intimate and personal manner. It is a growing market here. It is an event, and if the writer is a good speaker and can reach his audience, it can be a success.

Will all this affect the relationship between author and publisher?
I spend lots of time with writers because I love it. I like being near them. For me, the writing process is the most fascinating part of my job. What comes after, the part which is selling the book, is done in the most transparent way possible, and we try to make sure that the writer understands what we're doing. I remember Günter Grass told me once that all he needed was a table and paper. I asked him: how much does paper cost? How much does an advert in a newspaper cost? He didn't know. Most writers do not know how the market works and it is our duty to explain it to them. I think the solution is to have a closer relationship with the writer. Without writers, we would not exist.

When you read a manuscript, what makes you decide to publish it?
I want to learn something from it. If it is a novel, for example, I want to learn about the form of writing, about the theme it is dealing with; or I want it to charge what I call 'my pleasure batteries.' If I do not learn anything, I do not publish it. That is my priority: to learn, to enjoy. Of course, some publishers only take into account the commercial aspects of books. When they read, they do not read for the sake of reading, they read to see if a book has the necessary commercial ingredients... Samuel Pepys said: 'I do not want to die because there are 400 books I have yet to read. I want to die when I have read them all.' His words are heroic. But I am content with thinking that up to the last moment of my life I will have books to read.

You have written some beautiful lines on childhood, which 'sometimes sends me a postcard.' If you could send a postcard to the child you once were, about what he was going to encounter, what would you write?
I would tell him that if he has to choose between the world of books and the world of the countryside, he should choose the world of the countryside, the woods—to flee the city. Either you go to Athens or you stay in the countryside.

PERSONAL LIBRARY

1. Kafka, Franz. *Diaries*, Schocken, New York, 1998
2. Elias Canetti's Notes
3. Walser, Robert. *Jakob von Gunten*, The New York Review of Books, New York, 1999
4. Complete works by Georges Simenon
5. Proust, Marcel. *In Search of Lost Time*, Modern Library, New York, 2003
6. Benjamin, Walter. *Berlin Childhood around 1900*, Harvard University Press, Cambridge, USA, 2006
7. Heinrich von Kleist's Short Stories
8. Everything Friedrich Nietzsche wrote up to 1880
9. Svevo, Italo. *Zeno's Conscience*, Vintage Books, London, 2003
10. De Unamuno, Miguel. *Mist*, University of Illinois Press, Champaign, USA, 2000

PETER MAYER

Ex-President of Penguin Group and
President of Overlook Press

PUBLISHING IS A MATTER OF INSTINCT

Peter Mayer at one time was the President of Penguin, the classic publishing house which he transformed. He was there from 1978 until the end of 1997, traveling tirelessly from one office of this historic British brand to another; from New York to London and from there to New Delhi, Johannesburg, Toronto and Australia. About to turn 75, he is still in charge of his own publishing house, Overlook Press, which he started with his father and which he has transformed into a small but very competitive business. In recent months he has placed at the top of the *New York Times* bestsellers list a book that nobody else had noticed: *True Grit*, by Charles Portis, now catapulted to fame thanks to the Coen brothers movie. 'Publishing is a matter of instinct', he says. In fact, he started out on this trade of following his instinct when he was just over 20, alternating his work as a taxi driver with graduate studies. At Avon Books, as a beginner, he rediscovered a novel, *Call It Sleep* by Henry Roth. He convinced the directors at Avon to republish it, and it went on to sell a million copies after appearing on the front page of the New York Times. What he did at Penguin later was historic, and he continues now with the same energy. He works tirelessly awaiting the revolution, which he does not deny. It was often said of him that he was a guru, because he guessed where the winds were coming from. Now the winds are hurricanes.

There is a poem by your friend Michael Krüger, the German publisher, which says that childhood sends one postcards. They say you are a guru. What postcard would that guru have sent to the present Peter Mayer about the future of the publishing world?
He would have said that technology was going to be more important not for culture, but for the transmission of culture. And that guru would have paid more attention to people like Marshall McLuhan. What has happened is that the world is connected in a way we would never have imagined, for better and for worse, and success is no longer so much linked to the imaginative world as it is to information. Information is now more important than imagination. This saddens me. We have a big soup of information in front of us, but we are much less concentrated. In the 1990s, I was not aware that this was going to happen.

What impact does this have on the work of a publisher now?
Our work is changing. Our role is basically the same, but the effect is probably smaller. The public used to have confidence in the value of our brand, our name, and our experience and education. Now, although the public still needs those filters, less attention is paid to any credentials. Everyone can talk to anyone in the world, without filters—this is a democratic idea that eliminates our mediation, not necessarily always a good thing.

But there are still publishers...
What is happening radically affects our job. There are many books I can no longer publish because technology is going at breakneck

speed. It takes me between six months and one year to publish a book, but the information that book contains can be outdated before it is released. My role as a publisher is probably to publish less information than before. And by information, I don't mean only politics, I mean everything related to everyday life, health, etc. You have all this information on the Internet. If I want to cook chicken Kiev, I do not need a Russian recipe book, I can find the recipes on the Internet, and they are free. What type of content do we want? That is the question we have to ask ourselves.

We could conclude that fiction should be on the rise, as it does not seem to be affected so much by these technological changes...
Well, maybe not 100 per cent. But yes, it has more importance now than a century ago. And it is true that literary fiction and plays are less affected by new technologies. I work in a world of writers, agents, lorries that bring books back and forth, a world of bookshops and readers. And the culture of the bookshop will have to change, because there will be fewer bookshops, not more. And that decrease will affect cultural centres in our cities. Now, the cultural centres are inside our houses. The few remaining bookshops in Anglo-Saxon countries are large chains, and what they now sell most of are machines to read e-books on. But—how does all this change my job? If we print fewer copies per title, printing and publishing costs will rise and the retail price will have to go up. So, books will be more expensive and this will drive people to read more e-books. I must admit that e-books are very convenient. So that if you recommend a book to me now, I could take out my little machine, I would buy it this very moment and I would be reading it in half an hour. Isn't that amazing?

And what will happen to writers, to their agents?
As long as there are books as we know them, the famous writers

will continue selling physical books and e-books. And perhaps in greater quantities. The less well-known authors may not be able to publish books in the traditional manner. Perhaps they might only publish them as e-books, perhaps by themselves... That sounds great, right? But there will be no certification at all, the book will no longer say it is backed by Gallimard or Faber & Faber or Hanser... This does not only affect writers but a whole community, publishers, agents, bookshops, magazines, newspapers... Think about newspapers. We need newspapers to spread word of our books, but if fewer and fewer newspapers and magazines are being read, fewer people will read books. If people do not care about filters and certifications, we will have a different culture of books. There will always be those who seek excellence, but how do you identify where it is?

How do you?
I don't think blogs have much credibility, but I do believe in word of mouth, and this will become increasingly more important. Social networks will multiply and this is the kind of marketing that will occur. From bottom to top, not the other way around. Our advertising effort is now focused on awakening interest in certain blogs, because some of them do have credibility. Just as there are people who know the difference between blogs, so publishers also will have to learn to differentiate. A literary agent friend of mine has set up a lecture agency. He not only uses his own writers, but others' too. In the same way that the music industry has had to focus more on live concerts than on selling CD's, we who work in the world of books will have to do the same. Writers can be marketing tools themselves, if they are eloquent and interesting.

Michael Krüger says that in the near future, writers could become troubadours.
Yes, but what happens is that some of them do not sing so well.

And a troubadour travels. A writer who is not famous and cannot afford to travel, is going to find it hard to be a troubadour.

While other elements in the industry are wondering how the future will be, it seems that for writers it is not so important. Why?
Most writers, especially literary ones, will continue writing whatever happens to the industry. They need to write. Perhaps they will find it harder to make a living out of it, but they will continue to do it. Herman Melville continued writing despite the fact that his books were not selling. And he wrote *Moby Dick* and *Billy Budd* because his motivation was to write. From the point of view of a serious writer, literature will continue to be there. And if things go well for him, he may well earn more money than he would working with a publishing house as he does now. All money generated will be his; but if the book does not do well, the writer will make less. At present, it is the publisher who runs the risk, who supports and protects the writer.

What would you have said in the 1990s, if you had then had a crystal ball to look into this revolution which awaits the Gutenberg world?
I would have said: now, in the 1990s, marketing is very important. But in 2020 or 2030 it will be less significant. In 1995, I would have said distribution is essential; but it will not be so important in 2020, because it will be done differently. You have asked me how the changes affect my job. We do not know what is going to happen, but I do believe the value of the physical book will rise in a strange way. In the past 30 years, we have seen how the price for the production of books has come down a lot around the world. Cheaper paper, cheaper bindings... The effort of publishers has focused on profit margins and the public has ceased to give importance to printing quality. It may happen that the book, in its original and well cared for format, will arouse interest again. People will buy books again for the idea

of ownership. I think books will be made better, they will be looked after better, better produced. Because if they're made badly, nobody will buy them.

Are you better equipped for the future being a small publisher, as head of Overlook Press, as opposed to being head of a giant like Penguin?
I think that if you are Penguin you are closer to winning, because you will have an important backlist, and what people pay for is content. But in the case of e-books from Penguin or Gallimard, a new book published by them might not have the same advantages in the future as today. I think brands will be less important in the future. The author himself will become the brand. When I left Penguin and took charge of Overlook Press, I did not realise that such a small company would be so well positioned for the future. I do not think big publishing companies are going to disappear either, but I do think they will be publishing fewer books and will get their benefits from the sale of e-books. And publishing houses will no longer need so many people. Something unusual is happening in the case of Overlook. Our backlist makes up about 20 per cent to 30 per cent of our books. This percentage is higher than that of many larger publishing houses, and we spend more money in acquiring out of print books. For me, a book is new if nobody has read it.

Is the publishing world better equipped in terms of hacking?
The music industry tried to stop piracy, but couldn't. Young people think that if music is not a physical object it is free. Books, cinema, newspapers and magazines have taken note, and now more than ever content is monetised... Pirating books is not as worrying as in cinema. It happens more in some countries than others, because I believe they are not used to paying. Piracy is like stealing, but I do not think it is going to seriously affect this industry. What we will have to do is continue to identify valued content, editing it with dignity,

publishing it in any format... This will not change. People like books, they like buying them. What Gutenberg invented (black on white), is the best way of reading. It will be different when children who are now six or seven grow up. I have already seen digital books for children whose drawings move. We have to admit these changes are surprising and exciting.

Are we witnessing the decline of the book as a business?
I do not like talking just about the business. I think about the young Gabriel García Márquez or the young Mario Vargas Llosa, how they emerged. How do we launch today's young writers? And that takes us to the heart of what we do. The aim of a publishing house is not just to accumulate a catalogue; our aim is to be creative, discover works and sometimes improve them.

What will not change is the mystery that lies behind the success of a book. Gaston Gallimard, founder of the French publishing house, said that after 40 years of experience he could not tell what it is that takes a book to succeed...
It's true. There is an element of luck, but it's better to be lucky when you are young. Why? Because if you are lucky when you are older, you will have less time left to enjoy it... What you have to have is instinct, not only with a view to what sells, but for what will continue to do so in the future.

PERSONAL LIBRARY

1. Kafka, Franz. *The Castle*, Random House, New York, 2011
2. Mann, Thomas. *The Magic Mountain*, Vintage Books, London, 2011
3. Roth, Henry. *Call it Sleep*, Picador, New York, 2005
4. De Cervantes, Miguel. *Don Quixote*, Penguin Classics, New York, 2003
5. Eliot, George. *Middlemarch*, Oneworld Classics, London, 2011
6. Fitzgerald, F. Scott. *The Great Gatsby*, Scribner Classics, New York, 2004
7. García Márquez, Gabriel. *One Hundred Years of Solitude*, Harper Perennial Modern Classics, New York, 2006
8. The four novels by Thomas Wolfe
9. Levi, Primo. *If this is a Man*, Little, Brown Book Group, London, 2003
10. Faulkner, William. *The Sound and the Fury*, W.W. Norton, New York, 1993
11. Proust, Marcel. *In Search of Lost Time*, Random House, New York, 2012
12. Twain, Mark. *Huckleberry Finn*, Penguin Books, London, 2012
13. Tolstoy, Leo. *War and Peace*, Penguin Group, New York, 2012
14. Dostoyevsky, Fyodor. *The Brothers Karamazov*, Penguin Classics, New York, 2003
15. Bellow, Saul. *Herzog*, Penguin Books, London, 2007

BEATRIZ DE MOURA

Founder and Chief Director of Tusquets Editores

THE FATES THAT HAVE SHAPED BEATRIZ DE MOURA

Beatriz de Moura, Brazilian by origin and sentiment, an optimist and a realist, a pragmatic but also daring woman, who wears on her lapel the distinctive 'Q' of her publishing company, Tusquets, one of the most prestigious in the Spanish language. This 'Q' is what distinguishes her books as well as herself. It signals her taste for Quality – or, to put it another way, she publishes Quality. This attitude, which is a type of manifesto in favour of indispensable literature, has enabled Beatriz de Moura to maintain her independent criteria over 40 years in publishing, and has been fundamental for the careers of authors such as Milan Kundera, Jorge Semprún and Almudena Grandes, amongst other Spanish, Latin American and other foreign authors. Describing her relationship with her writers, all of them evidently complex, is like composing a style book to illustrate what a traditional publisher means to writers. Will this relationship that Beatriz de Moura represents change with the advent of the technological tsunami? Are we talking about a unique publisher, like others of her type or generation – Jorge Herralde, Peter Mayer, Inge Feltrinelli, Antoine Gallimard...? Will the 'Q' of her brand continue to be essential in understanding the author's (and reader's) fidelity to a chosen publisher? She is elegant and daring, but also prudent. She says that in revolutions such as this one, which affect the future of books as we have known them, she steps back and waits. And, she continues, she waits with the authors, armed and ready to embrace a new future dimension, that looks set to become an opportunity instead of a menace, with the spirited enthusiasm she shares with her team, and shared above all with her partner Toni López, now sadly non longer with us. This conversation, which includes valuable insights regarding her professional relationships, reveals the adventurous and fortunate career of a committed publisher who has consolidated her prestige through the favourable circumstances of life.

What was the spark that made you become a publisher?
One must go back to my childhood. My father was an avid reader; he had a very complete library. Since he was a diplomat, we moved to different countries every two or three years, so I was educated in several countries, in several languages, in various cultures... The only thing that was reproduced in the same way every time we moved, whatever the city, whatever the place in the world, was my father's library. As a result, my first home, my only home in fact, was that library.
Perhaps that is why, as far back as I can remember, I wished to live surrounded by books. This was perhaps the fertile ground in which the seed of the future publisher sprouted. Nevertheless, what's certain is that it is really due to the swings of fate across time.

And how does fate work?
By one's *modus vivendi*. When I was studying in Geneva in the 1950s, I took advantage of my diplomatic passport and my SEAT 600 to help different anti-Francoist groups. My father found out and kicked me out of the house. He saw me as a problem and tried to force me to abandon Geneva and my studies. He must have thought I would immediately return to my comfortable life as a daddy's girl. But he didn't foresee that two stubborn people rarely give in. The first twist of fate. So I had to learn to survive and earn a living. After finishing my studies in spite of all obstacles, I returned to Barcelona, where I decided to live permanently, and I looked for a job. And then came the second swing of fate: fortune would have it that I would begin working in the mornings as a translator at the Gustavo Gili publishing house. At that time, it was exclusively an art and technical publishing house, though

they also published adventure novels such as *Tarzan* by Edgar Rice Burroughs. I was asked to translate a famous German book on architecture, known amongst professionals as *Neufert*, from Spanish into Portuguese. Soon afterwards, I was employed at Salvat in the afternoons collaborating on a literary encyclopaedia. It goes without saying that I extended my work hours past the limits of decency. To complement my two salaries, I translated as much as I could in the evenings for other publishers, with or without pseudonyms.

Involved with books all day long. But one thing is wanting to have a close proximity to books, and quite another is the bureaucracy of publishing, translation...
That plurality of jobs, which lasted for three or four years, was purely to feed myself. Around about 1964, a girl named Esther Tusquets, who was about to found a publishing house called Lumen, phoned me. She wanted me to translate the albums of the *Topo Gigio* series, a delightful little Italian television creature that became very famous throughout the whole world at the time. Soon afterwards, Esther felt that I could work at Lumen with a full time salary, doing a bit of everything. Suddenly I was aware that my situation was a unique and unrepeatable opportunity to learn the skills that could one day lead me to what I had always dreamed of – that is, of living surrounded by books. I left all my other jobs, despite earning considerably less, and immersed myself body and soul in what was expected of me. And I tried to do it as well as I could.
Esther created a collection of fiction, *Palabra en el Tiempo*, which was directed by Professor Antonio Vilanova. Working beside her, I learned, little by little and with time, how by means of coherent literary criteria one forms what is now known as an editorial style. I began selecting the manuscripts and foreign books they had requested or received by chance, and adapted my own preferences to theirs. I learned that when you work for someone else, it is important

to respect the criteria of those who choose and decide what books to publish. It cost me a lot to repress some of my enthusiasms, and I was humbled on more than one occasion, perhaps rightly so. The fact is that Esther and her father, Magín Tusquets, knew how to create and run in the 1960s one of the most prestigious publishing companies in the Spanish language, and I am grateful to them for having had me at their side during their first five years.

In a world where publishing was very European, very mature, you see Carlos Barral, who was still a boy, Esther herself, with Jorge Herralde arriving on the scene, and Josep Maria Castellet who was also somewhere around... It was a time when the big publishers' names in Spain began to become renowned despite their youth. There was a climate which seemed to favour it.

When Esther founded her publishing house around 1964, Carlos Barral had already been working in his family's old printing press and publishing house, Seix Barral, for nine years. And Castellet had already started working at Edicions 62, where he was—and continues to be 50 years later—the point of reference. At the same time, the historic publishing houses already in existence, especially in Catalonia, which was and still is the heart of the publishing industry, began to open up to the world, perhaps encouraged by the presence (when censorship was still as grotesque as it was severe) of a very slight cosmopolitan air tinged with a fragile permissiveness. Within this same atmosphere, Tusquets Editor appeared, founded by myself and the architect Oscar Tusquets, my ex-husband and Esther's brother. Also in 1969, Jorge Herralde, an engineer who came from his family's factory, founded Anagrama. We were the youngest publishers of the Spanish publishing world for many years.

I believe we had the intuition—and along with us, many who were also in their thirties—that we could no longer count on a revolution that had never happened, nor ever would happen, and that like it or not, the dictator would end up dying in bed like any other normal citizen. Intuitively, almost in the manner of survivors, we decided, without exactly giving it articulate expression, not to fall into the despondency and discouragement that had, in contrast, undermined the morale of so many talented and brilliant people of the generation previous to ours. Besides, when you are as young and intellectually arrogant as we were then, you believe you can do anything and everything and that the future is all yours.

Back then you had a vocation as a publisher, working at Lumen and surrounded by masters like Carlos Barral, Josep Maria Castellet... What did you learn from them and what remains from that learning process?
Everything. That long and passionate learning process was the foundation of a vocation that only then did I discover was gestating within me. I learned a great deal, not only in the daily work but also in the vocational part, from the successes and failures of great publishers like Carlos Barral, Giulio Einaudi, Giangiacomo Feltrinelli, Jerôme Lindon, Jean-Jacques Pauvert or Barney Rosset, Beckett's publisher in the United States. It was clear to me that without the fighting and cosmopolitan spirit that moved all of them, my incipient vocation was unlikely to become a true commitment in a very demanding trade.

When did you decide to go independent?
I didn't decide. Esther decided for me. And this is the third swing of fate. I proposed the creation of two collections within Lumen of famous short texts (between 80 and 100 pages long), which I put together later on, known to this day as 'the silver' (*Cuadernos Ínfimos*) and 'the golden' (*Cuadernos Marginales*) notebooks. Esther probably thought these collections would not work in Lumen. For whatever reason, she didn't wish to publish them, or couldn't, or didn't feel like it. In fact, every publisher is free to choose what they publish.

I was hurt by the way she disregarded me, but am convinced that this was the best thing that could have happened to me.

Behind you there is a sign that reminds me of something Peter Mayer always quotes: 'From the start, say no.'
Maybe that's why I have that little sign visible on the shelf, as a warning for everyone to see. The fact is, from the moment of that silent and enigmatic negation, Oscar and I found support amongst friends and acquaintances who began collaborating, sometimes just 'for the love of art', suggesting texts, translating or editing them. It was a time of tremendous euphoria and effervescent creativity, also of great camaraderie, that I'll never, ever forget.

You continued in Lumen and with your own publishing company?
No, not any more. It wasn't possible; the situation pointed to an irredeemable incompatibility. So, with the modest economic investment of the brother and father of my former boss, I moved on to a new chapter in my life!

How did you feel?
The way you always feel when you begin something for the very first time: panicky. I felt terror. Terror at not knowing how capable or not I was of carrying out a rather risky project with a tiny economic investment. But I am a very obstinate and very persistent person. I admit it wasn't easy; at times I even reached the point of throwing in the towel. I ask myself today how much time in my life as a publisher has been dedicated to reading books, and how much to dealing with financial problems. I am unable to answer this clearly. At the beginning of the 1970s, thanks to some minor success and taking advantage of a more relaxed censorship, we created Acracia, a collection of free-thinking authors comprising larger volumes and some more expensive translations. This collection had

152

some success in helping us maintain an unstable equilibrium, but an equilibrium nonetheless.

In the spring of 1973, I met Antonio López Lamadrid, a businessman from the textile industry who, oddly enough, was in the midst of changing his life, having just abandoned his business and taken a year off to find a new and more gratifying livelihood. One day, after the dictator had died, it occurred to me to ask him to look at the accounts at Tusquets, and perhaps counsel me on how to improve its financial situation, as things didn't get off to the best start. He gave me the best advice he was ever to give me: to transform this minute company into a public limited company with new shareholders and more capital that would guarantee its future. Oscar and Magín Tusquets, his father (the founding shareholders of this publishing company), were enthused by the idea, and so Tusquets Editores, in the plural, was born, with six more partners, including Antonio – known as Toni López from then on in the publishing world and amongst his new friends and partners.

For 14 years, these eight partners placed their trust in my criteria and in the literary decisions which they never questioned, not even in the years when the company was not yet producing dividends, or when reinvesting profits did not seem inconvenient. They were admirable, exceptional. I will always be grateful to them.

You were the one who was doing the work.
Yes, I was doing the work, but I worked under privileged conditions with total professional freedom, as I believe no one else in this country has been able to who hasn't happened to be the owner of her company. In fact, it has taken me 25 years or more to become a shareholder myself. It's true that, alongside me, Toni had already begun to organise the whole business framework of the company with enthusiasm and imagination, relieving me of a very heavy load. I think we formed an unequalled tandem, similar to the one formed

by Víctor Seix and Carlos Barral or, perhaps, Magín and Esther Tusquets. We never, in more than 20 years, made a decision without first consulting one another, although sometimes at the expense of long and complicated discussions. But Toni was able to create what I still call 'the smallest multinational in the world', with subsidiaries of Tusquets in Mexico and Argentina as well as a reasonable distribution network throughout most of Latin America.

And so, already equipped with the collection of erotic literature, La Sonrisa Vertical, which was selling very well...

It was the moment.
Exactly. It coincided with the explosion of joy at the death of Franco and that period of euphoric blooming of practically all the freedoms, now known as the transition.

La Sonrisa Vertical, in fact, emerged in the midst of this euphoria. But above all it was thanks to the creation of the Andanzas narrative collection that we began the 1980s prepared for a new stage, in which we took various risks that luckily turned out very well for us. It was, in fact, a definitive period for the consolidation of the publishing company. I began to take an interest in books that belonged to a very different market from the one we had dealt with up until then. All the international publishers that had shown their support towards our work throughout the years came back once again to support us, and this time with less fear of being mistaken, given that we were paying more and sooner. We were able to choose more important authors, because we were beginning to be more competitive.

The Andanzas collection was not only born of an old desire of mine, but also above all out of a business necessity. Because of its format, its innovative design (back then practically no one gave much importance to the cover design), and its first books, in which either an author (a Nobel Prize winner such as Czeslaw Milosz) provided a certain prestige or a work (*A Princess in Berlin*, by an unknown author) ensured good sales, all contributed to preparing the terrain for the great leap of faith we took in 1984 and 1985, when Toni and I had to confront one of those moments in which you know you have to risk everything if you really believe your project is worth it. In fact, I remember three almost consecutive moments in less than six or eight months, in which everyone would have said we were out of our minds. Moments which we really didn't look for, but which looked for us, decisive moments. I still remember Toni's wild gaze—he always relished the vertigo of the hazardous—when he asked me, 'Are you willing to take the risk?' and myself, feeling somewhat dizzy, thinking that what was being proposed was worth it, replying: 'Alright, yes! Forward!' as if we were staking our life on it. Between the summer of 1984 and the spring of 1985 we contracted the following books for sums we had never handled before: *The Lover*, by Marguerite Duras, *The Unbearable Lightness of Being*, by Milan Kundera and *The World According to Garp*, by John Irving, and consequently we became the publishers of these authors in Spanish.

The Lover came to us directly from Jérôme Lindon, the publisher at Éditions de Minuit; he offered it to us, warning us in an almost paternal way that, if we were to let the opportunity pass, we would be, quite simply, fools. He was right, of course. A short time later, we got wind of Milan Kundera's much anticipated great novel, *The Unbearable Lightness of Being*, through someone who had just visited him in Paris and implied that we might be able to 'seduce' him. Two days later, we were at the door of his then tiny apartment. On the other hand, we owe Irving's novels indirectly to Severiano Ballesteros. We had promised Irving's agent in London that if he gave us something special, we would give him an autographed golf ball from the champion. And so it happened: Toni, who knew him, got the autograph for the agent, and we got John Irving!

Before going to see the Kunderas—Milan and Vera, his wife—I bought his first three books translated into Spanish, which I had already read in French. I quickly perused fragments of each one of them; I discovered a very different Kundera from the one I knew in French. My first impression was that I liked his style much more in Spanish than in French.

Was the translation directly from Czech into Spanish?
Yes, Fernando Valenzuela has always translated directly from the Czech Kundera's work written in his mother tongue.

Who published him?
Seix Barral. The fact is, knowing he was open to the idea of changing his publisher in Spain, we lost no time and very cautiously approached his apartment in Paris. Right from the start, they were extremely pleasant and welcoming. Milan asked which of us two was the editor. When I told him it was me, he took me aside by the arm, leaving Toni with Vera. From that very moment on, our many professional encounters followed the same ritual: I conversed with Milan about questions related to the texts, and Toni dealt with financial matters with Vera. Then we would have an *eau-de-vie* whilst standing in the kitchen, before going to a restaurant of their choice. During that first encounter, he asked me suddenly: 'What do you think of the Spanish translations of my books?' I told him that I couldn't give a proper opinion, because I didn't read Czech and, therefore, could only compare it with the French translations. 'And which translations do you prefer?' he asked, to my surprise. I admitted enjoying the Spanish versions more. He became livid: 'And why?' He insisted. I told him that the French versions reminded me of classic French authors who wrote long sentences and paragraphs and above all employed an excessive adjectivisation, which was not the case in the Spanish versions. The rhythm of the Spanish versions was of course more syncopated, and the punctuation was richer and particularly expressive.

Wasn't he aware of this?
In those days he wasn't able to be.

He didn't speak French?
He spoke beginner's French and couldn't really form a serious opinion, although something must have seemed bizarre to him, otherwise he wouldn't have asked. He was very grateful to his French publisher not only for being the first in the world to publish him, but also for making him known internationally. He then confessed to me: 'What you've just told me leaves me perplexed.' He said no more. A little later, he called Vera over, they talked together in Czech and she turned to me and said: 'You have won my husband over! You've touched on a matter that is now fundamental for him.' I sat still, looking at Toni in astonishment, while Vera started asking him for catalogues and all possible information about us. Milan told us he had just finished a new novel in Czech, and asked us for Fernando Valenzuela's address.

And did you come to an agreement?
Until now, the ritual has always been the same. When he began writing in French, he didn't even let me decide, he imposed himself: 'From now on I want you to translate me.' I said: 'I'm not sure I'll have the time.' 'Don't worry, I'll wait', he replied, knowing perfectly well that in any case we would be in more of a hurry than him to publish a new book of his. Well, alright, since then I have been delighted to translate his books written in French. I think they truly enjoyed our visits, and our outings together, Toni and myself, and the two of them, to those places, so very *Mitteleuropa*, and so very much them. We would go to Paris...

To the Pont Royal.
No. We never went to the Pont Royal, next to the Gallimard offices,

because we had no money back then. With time, we would end up going to the Lutetia, which is equally expensive, but always with a table and is nearer to their house.

Along with *The Lover* by Marguerite Duras, you had two successes in a row.
Almost in a row.

Which one came out first?
The Lover, in 1984. *The Unbearable Lightness of Being*, in 1985. Toni and I went to Paris while Ana María Moix translated *The Lover*, as I was preoccupied with finding the right illustration for the cover of a novel of such a kind, which we wanted to publish as soon as possible. In France it was a best-seller practically the day it came out. It occurred to me that the best image would be one of the author herself in the Mekong Delta at the time when the novel took place. I called her, asked her what she thought of my idea, and she answered that she would look through her old photographs and then let me know. In fact, she called, with that well-known hoarse and sleepy voice of hers, and said to me: *'Venez! Il y a tout un gros tiroir de photos. Vous piocherez dedans'* ('Come! There's a whole drawer of photos. You can rummage through them'). We went, Toni and I, and searched through them in silence – her silence, the eloquent silence of an ex-alcoholic. Suddenly, this photo of a young girl appeared...

The photo on the cover.
Exactly. The one that later appeared on every cover after ours of all the editions the world over. The only one she herself decided was adequate. When the film was made afterwards, it turned out that the actress who played the role of the young girl in the novel looked just like the adolescent Duras of the photo. It was striking. When I asked her during our first encounter if she liked the photo, she said:

'Yes, but it's not me. Look at me, what kind of a face do I have now? What do you think of my face?'

Her present face?
Yes, you know, her face as an old woman. Then, borrowing an expression she used to describe herself, written I can't remember where, I said: 'I see a face *dévastée*.' And, yes, so it was, she had a completely worn out, demolished face, as if history had run her over, devastating her. 'Fine. That, in fact, is how it is', she said. And I took the original photo of the young girl. She didn't ask us for money, she didn't ask us for anything. We later returned the photograph.

What does one feel in a moment like that?
You feel like kissing her on the mouth, that admirable old woman destroyed by life, by alcohol, by solitude, an immense and bottomless solitude.

Of course, you are obtaining something which will transform the book into a much more appealing object. That is the publisher's role.
Yes, that and other things as well...

And then it was book after book and success after success.
Meanwhile, with greater solvency, we had already begun the process of publishing Spanish language authors. In fact, we had already tried at the very beginning with authors such as Enrique Vila-Matas, whose first two books were included in the collection *Cuadernos Íntimos*. At the end of the 1970s, we were pleased to present the first book of short stories by Cristina Fernández Cubas. Later on, in the mid 1980s, we discovered to our amazement Eduardo Mendicutti, with a magnificent book of erotic stories, *Seven Against Georgia*, who was a finalist for La Sonrisa Vertical prize. We've just finished publishing his thirteenth novel, *Mae West y yo*.

To me he would have to be one of the great writers that have emerged from the Spanish transition to the democracy.

And Almudena Grandes.
Yes, Almudena Grandes won that same prize in 1989 with her famous *The Ages of Lulu*, translated into 24 languages. Well then, that same year we published a totally unknown novelist whose manuscript appeared out of the large number of original manuscripts that were then being sent to us. After a first reading, I received the manuscript; it took me a while to read it, because it was long, it was written on a typewriter without spacing between the lines, and, as if that wasn't enough, it was interspersed with tiny handwritten corrections. That is how our reading was before the computer... and how great writers were born without the need for many other tools. I started reading the manuscript with an enormous indolence, but after a few pages, I couldn't put it down. It was *Juegos de la edad tardía* by Luis Landero.
Before getting to the middle of the novel I thought to myself: 'This rumpled manuscript has surely been seen by other publishers'. I started to tremble. 'I can't believe someone has read this and not kept it.' I called the author—Luis still remembers this story clearly—and I told him of my interest. He told me to finish reading his novel calmly, because it had either been rejected by some or he simply hadn't received an answer from others. I finished it calmly, because in a way I had already accomplished a difficult task. You know the rest of the story: as of today we have published his eight books in the span of 22 years. *Juegos de la edad tardía* has become a classic.

And it continues being read.
Exactly. Imagine how important that year was for us... I remember three great enthusiasts for Almudena's novel in the jury of La Sonrisa Vertical prize.

Hortelano?

Juan García Hortelano, our dear ambassador in Madrid, and/or the reverse... That's how we knew him in Catalonia. In fact we all fell in love with that novel. I thought to myself emotionally: it's not only a clear winner of the prize, but it's also the novel of a well-formed writer. And, in effect, her literary trajectory is proof of the unusual force she had already manifested. Throughout these 21 years, I have never ceased to be amazed by the power of her imagination and the solid importance of all her work. Now, nothing coming from her surprises me. When she told Toni some four or five years ago about the project she was undertaking, I immediately made a mental calculation of how old I would be when she completed the sixth and last volume of those *Episodios de una guerra interminable*. Maybe I'm being a bit rash saying this here, but I plan to assist in its gestation and publication whatever happens. Furthermore, I promised her so, now that Toni is no longer here. It's extraordinary, in the 21st century, to have the privilege of supporting and publishing an author who plans on dedicating the next ten years of her life to the creation of a work such as this...

A saga.

No, it's not a saga! I'd say it's a fresco. Six frescos of Francoist Spain in its early years, those which the regime so cynically named 25 years of Peace. The first instalment, *Inés y la alegría*, was published last year and has been a success. We will publish the second, *El lector de Julio Verne*, in March of 2012.

But we had left off where, by the beginning of the 1990s, Tusquets had overcome its survival phase to enter into that of definitive consolidation. However, I'm not sure why, every time I feel my life is entering a relaxed phase, something occurs that puts me on the alert. In 1994, an impending crisis of a moderate nature pushed one of our oldest and most faithful shareholders to think about

selling his shares, which had already risen in value. And, as if in-
fected by a contagious fear, all the other shareholders wanted to
sell theirs as well. The company was functioning perfectly well, but
Toni and I didn't have enough capital to buy all the shares and become the sole owners. Planeta bought 49 per cent of the company
with the written commitment to sell its stake to us two years later
if we wished to buy it. And two years later we did just that. I must
praise José Manuel Lara Bosch once again for his conduct: not only
did he strictly respect the terms of the contract with exceptional
savoir faire and loyalty, but he also warned us that we were about
to make a big mistake. And, in effect, we did. Two or three years
later, we had our fingers burnt and withdrew from a 50 per cent
partnership with RBA, whose owner doesn't even deserve mention
here, or anywhere... a most undesirable person...
There was a return to times of great uncertainty. To buy our economic
independence by means of a bank loan was only made possible by
the fact that the company was, for the moment, quite frankly hum-
ming along, and because now Toni and I, being the only shareholders,
decided not to make any further mistakes...

And now Tusquets Editores is truly yours?
Come on, don't put it like that, because it isn't that certain!

How do you feel having told this story?
Well, perfectly fine. I have felt very comfortable telling it. Why?

I mean, it's a story of a vocation that becomes a success. You insisted
on becoming a publisher ever since that initial spark, furthermore,
you've contracted authors you have liked to read and now you are one
of the most important publishers in the world.
I don't feel that way. The publishing business is not what it was just
15 years ago, and tomorrow it will be different, and of course, in

these times either we have to adapt or die in the effort to continue in this trade. In this new world, a publishing company like ours can't survive in the mid-term if it continues using business models from the past under present day circumstances. Society has changed not only as a result of the technological tsunami which has brought new entertainments, distractions and sources of information. The social changes are extremely profound. Habits, the educational system, material priorities above those of intellect and knowledge, have all changed. Reading is no longer a priority. In France, there are legions of so-called 'illiterates', or those who read, but don't understand what they're reading... In this situation, those of us who continue reading and publishing books on paper—as well as other formats, whatever they may be, but basically on paper—must, as I was saying, exercise our trade in such a way that it may continue despite everything, despite the too hasty optimists; so that it doesn't lose its essence, which has always been and will continue to be indispensable for the development of the human intellect: learning and thinking.

The structure of book retailing has also changed. The distribution systems of just five years ago are already showing signs of fatigue, and sooner rather than later will become obsolete.

And, well, perhaps one day I will become, as you say, one of the great publishers of the world, but that still remains to be seen. I still lack something. I must still find a way, in the midst of this *revolú* (mess), as a female Puerto Rican writer would say, to make Tusquets Editores survive these times in *bellezza* without losing its essential traits. That is the challenge now. I cannot let my eye wander, or allow myself distractions or relaxation. That is what engages me now. If I don't achieve that, I will not consider myself a 'great publisher.'

There is something else which is difficult to bequeath, the spirit you yourself have been creating. How would you summarise that spirit?
I'd say now that it is the spirit of someone who wishes to grow old

without losing the curiosity and ardour (what a great word!) of her youth and her maturity. For the time being, I feel I maintain it without making too much of a fool of myself.

In what way has the figure of the publisher changed, how is it changing now and what makes it change?
The figure of the publisher as I understood and represented it when I started working in this trade has changed with time except, perhaps, in the case of the many small publishing houses that luckily have been proliferating in Spain and around the world. In these cases, the publisher is the owner of his business as well as the instigator of an editorial line. At the same time, however, publishers have appeared who work for others, as is the case with those who are the creative part in brands inside large publishing companies where the owners are often unknown. In English, they are distinguished by two very different words: the publisher is the owner or owners, and the editor is the creator with his team working together in preparing the manuscripts, translations, etc. With this development, I see myself best portrayed as an editor. But since I have become a shareholder, and above all since Toni's death, I am inevitably both an editor and a publisher.

You've introduced an editorial line which is...?
The one that defines the Tusquets Editores trademark, and that the reader recognises.

And the French designer who attached so much importance to the illustration and to the Tusquets trademark on the cover was right.
He was right.

People must remember the brand. Finally – books as we know them today, in coexistence with books in new formats; do you see a difficult battle or is it a battle to which you see a solution?

Not only do I see a solution, but we've already taken all the necessary steps so that precisely, when the right moment arrives (I emphasise this, because it is not a detail – it is now the essence of the question), not only are we prepared to avoid having to fight the controlled and full implementation of new digital formats, but, on the contrary, we are prepared to use digital technology in the marketing of the traditional book in paper format as well as of books in digital formats. I'm 72 years old and I know I won't be around to witness the end of this evolution, but I will see a good part of it, as in fact I already am.

And will the physical book survive this attack?
I could be wrong, but I'm convinced it will. A time will come when reading in either format will have become a matter of indifference.

And in which do you prefer to read?
Well, of course, as a reader who simply reads for pleasure, I like to read the classic book in its tangible and valuable paper format. As a publisher, on the other hand, I have no problem reading in any of the digital formats. I can move around with five or more books in my suitcase without weighing it down, which is important.

Do you read online?
If you are referring to whether I visit Facebook, Twitter or some of the thousand and one other blogs in the world, I admit I don't. I don't have time for that. On the other hand, others have no time to read...

So, you are already tempted by the novelty.
Not tempted. I'm deeply involved.

And both formats will coexist.
I firmly believe so. No one can predict the future, especially this future that depends on so many factors. Whoever thinks he can, in

addition to being intellectually arrogant, runs the risk of making a fool of himself. No mode of expression has disappeared because of the advent of another. It is in the logic of things, and history has amply demonstrated that human beings, in addition to being gregarious, are accumulative.

PERSONAL LIBRARY

1. Hergé. *The Adventures of Tintin,* Little, Brown Books for Young Readers, New York, 2008
2. Twain, Mark. *The Adventures of Tom Sawyer,* Oxford University Press, Oxford, 2008
3. Swift, Jonathan. *Gulliver's Travels,* Penguin Classics, London, 2003
4. May Alcott, Louisa. *Little Women,* Penguin Classics, New York, 2010
5. Everything Jane Austen ever wrote
6. Stendhal. *The Charterhouse of Parma,* Oxford University Press, Oxford, 2009
7. Camus, Albert. *The Outsider,* Penguin Classics, New York, 2000
8. Chandler, Raymond. *Farewell, My Lovely,* Penguin Books, London, 2009
9. Ellison, Ralph. *Invisible Man,* Vintage Books, New York, 1995
10. James, Henry. *The Aspern Papers,* HardPress Publishing, Lenox, USA, 2010

STEPHEN PAGE
Publisher and CEO of Faber & Faber

BIG PUBLISHING HOUSES HAVE TO RESTRUCTURE
THEMSELVES IN ORDER TO SURVIVE

It must be very pleasurable and very frightening, to be sitting here in this publishing house built on the genius of T. S. Eliot, one of the greatest writers of the 20th century. Eliot has left his mark on Faber & Faber, the great English publishing house for literature. This has been as decisive in sustaining its prestige as it has been fundamental in sustaining it financially. The success of the musical *Cats*, which was based on Eliot's *Old Possum's Book of Practical Cats*, was instrumental in preserving the objectives of Eliot and his companions: to maintain within the legendary Bloomsbury a publishing company that would make money gambling on a catalogue which would not make the founders turn in their graves.

The person occupying this position and trying to fulfil that mission is Stephen Page (British-born in 1965), a publisher who had several experiences in commercial publishing before arriving at this sanctuary. Two recent examples speak of his success in his relationships with the writers, which is the key to Faber & Faber: Harold Pinter asked him to represent him at the reception of the Nobel Prize he was awarded, and P. D. James, the great lady of detective fiction, outlined in a dedication the devotion editors and publishing houses sometimes bestow on their writers. 'To Stephen Page, publisher, and to all my friends, old and new, at Faber & Faber.'

This is a weighty duty, especially in a publishing house that bases itself on the relationship between writer and publisher, but it has enabled them to create a backlist which is second to none.

You are running a publishing house founded by people who had a great respect for books of the past, especially for poetry. How do you deal with that history and the world that confront us?

Here, you feel and acknowledge the 80 years of legacy of Faber & Faber, the pragmatism with which people led this company and the backlist they created. However, the catalogue is not the only thing they created, there is an identity with poetry at its centre, which was a gamble. Faber & Faber has always been a publishing house spanning many genres: ranging from children's books to gardening. The archives are full of quality commercial books and for that reason, Faber & Faber has been able to survive and remain independent. And for this reason it has managed to publish extraordinary writers and works. We have a great history, but you cannot wake up every morning thinking that you must publish the new *Waste Land* by T. S. Eliot. Although you may always wake up with the hope that one of the works you publish has a great impact in the future and will be able to contribute to that overwhelming backlist.

How has your own experience helped you to run a publishing house like this one?

My personal background has created a strange mixture of experience and interests that seem made-to-measure for managing Faber & Faber. I have never been an editor. I have always been in the commercial sphere, in small publishing houses or in big ones. However, in the course of my life I have always been a passionate reader. Now at Faber & Faber I have a group of extraordinary editors who are experts in their field. My job as publisher consists of supervising them, but I am not one of them. It is crucial that the role of publishing is closely related to the purely editorial work. Coming from a commercial background I learned that being close to the market did not mean you knew what would work. You may know many things, but you can never predict what is going to happen to a work once it is released on the market. The commercial aspect in the publishing world is overvalued. We do not know the changes that approach, so we cannot predict if a book is going to be a success or not. What happened yesterday may not be important tomorrow.

Was there an exact moment when you realised this?
From 1995 on, the UK market became fierce. Publishers treated the work, the packaging and the marketing with more care than ever. But that is not enough. You have to be attentive to the way the market works without letting it dictate what you have to publish or how.

How was Faber & Faber able to resist this tough market?
At Faber & Faber, we are lucky to be able to count on extraordinary shareholders who understand that literature is a long-term game with ups and downs. The company is owned half by the Faber & Faber family, half by a trust on behalf of T. S. Eliot's widow, Valerie Eliot. They are not expecting miracles to occur from one day to the next. They understand that there must be a balance between the identity of the company and what it publishes. Here, we know that if we have excellent copyrights, and look after what we publish and hold fast to our objectives, that will create success in the long term. We must strongly believe in quality and gamble on it. We believe in the large number of readers who want something of quality.

The Internet has burst into current book culture. How do you see the future of books and bookshops? Are they in danger of dying?
Both the writer and the reader are in very good health, and that is

the essence of our business. Although yes, there are many changes regarding the way we conduct it. However, I'm optimistic. Our job consists of making sure that what the writers write is of excellent quality and making sure it reaches the readers. That is our job. One concern among publishers was that writers would go directly to readers without going through the publishing house. Some have, but many haven't. The investment in writers has not vanished. Publishing houses exist to invest in writers, and this will continue. The second step, which is editing, improving what is written, is still something that is done to a deep level here at Faber & Faber. And the investment in this part of the business is considerable. At least, that's how it should be. The publishing houses have to serve the writer, not the other way round. I know agents and writers who believe that publishing houses don't try hard enough in this, and in some cases, it is true. This is dangerous, because without a doubt the best investment is the one made in the writer. The third step is to get to the reader. Now we have new competitors, like Amazon. Some believe that Amazon knows who the reader is and publishing houses don't; that we know the bookshops but not the readers. There is truth in this and that's why publishing houses are starting to transform themselves, aiming more at the reader and depending less on the places where the books are sold. Mass-market publishing houses had a monopoly in the sense that they controlled how the books made their way to the bookshops, supermarkets or general stores. However, they don't have that monopoly any more and don't control how digital books get to the reader. In the United Kingdom, digital sales are predicted to be 20 per cent of our income in a year or two. Another 20 per cent we will sell through Amazon and similar companies. That represents 40 per cent of income that won't come from bookshops. For me, that is a great threat: how do you restructure the system so as to make sure the bookshops continue to exist. But, as I said before, I firmly believe that readers will keep buying printed books, and although there is more and more demand for digital books, printed books won't follow the same course as music, for instance.

Why?
A CD is a CD... Not a book. The book continues to be an object. 30 per cent of books are bought as gifts. The age of most music purchasers is young; the buyers of books are older. Most books are bought by men and women who are more than 50 years old. That said, I think that what is important is that people should read. I don't care if it's an e-book. What we may need to do is produce more seductive, more attractive books.

Are you worried about free downloading?
Of course. If you speak to anyone who works in the recording world, their principal concern is piracy, as they call it. The copyright licensors have to guarantee the protection of the writer and his work. That license has to work so that the writer's work will not be abused, because if the license system doesn't protect him, everything will break down. The problem in the digital world is that there exists a thin line between the use and abuse of the work. One of the greatest pleasures is to lend books to our friends. If I lend the book *To Kill a Mockingbird* by Harper Lee to a friend, I don't feel bad about it because he didn't pay a royalty to the writer for reading it. But we have to think of a new way to operate with the digital world. We have to make people aware that the only source of income for a writer is the copyright.

I thought I had come to speak to a businessman in the publishing industry, and I discover that you preserve a certain editorial romanticism: the value of the writer, the value of the bookshop, the value of the well-produced book...
I'm a romantic businessman! If you reviewed the history of the

publisher's job, there will always be a romantic and intuitive side. I would like to think that our job must continue being about our close relationship to the writer. We have to keep creating strong bonds with the writer, the bookseller and the reader. At the same time, we have to learn the new market and to share in an equitable manner. I would like more than ever to strengthen the bonds with the writer. We have people from 20 to 65 years old working at Faber & Faber, and in the last years we have brought in younger people. This has proved quite interesting and it's important to listen to them. It's necessary to know what they think and how they operate, as they represent consumers of the future, and they are different.

What have you learned at a personal level from this job which is to be the editor of the editors?
It is not about liking everything an editor proposes, but if he defends a work with zeal, you have to pay attention. It's a job that requires balance. On the one hand, you have to protect the long-term relationship with the writer whilst opening windows and creating opportunities for new writers. Evaluation is also necessary. Editors aren't necessarily the best people for judging the price of copyright. The commercial department has a significant role to play here. It's not there to judge the work or to say that they don't want to buy it. Their job consists of saying 'OK, we want this work, how much is it worth on the market?' It's a matter of finding the balance between the commercial side and the editorial side. Coming from the commercial world, it's perhaps easy for me to speak to them.

T. S. Eliot once said: 'A literary critic should have no emotions except those immediately provoked by a work of art.' Is this applicable to the editor?
Yes, of course. You have to keep a certain mental clarity, but without doubt the most important thing is to be driven by passion and

judgement of quality. In no other department of a publishing house does one live so close to the creation of the work. To be an editor involves being as close as possible to the writer. And that is exciting. You need to know what they need, how they feel. Of course, there are some other important issues to talk about with the writer, such as commercial and legal aspects, but that is not the job of the editor.

Gallimard said that the publisher is someone who dares to choose and who knows how to wait. He said that this was the golden rule.
He is right. And I would add the word gamble. You have to gamble. Because this is a chaotic universe. You can't tell the writer to write in a particular way or give them absurd delivery dates. Writers work in a different way. We have to work with what we are given. Sometimes you receive more than you need. Sometimes less. So you have to maintain a level of calm. Because there are far more failures than successes. You have to learn from the failures. This industry generally attracts very critical people. So we have to remain calm. We don't know what we're going to receive or when. And when we do receive it, we have to see where it's going to take us. There's nothing concrete.

As Gallimard said, 'If you speak with certainty of a book, you are not a publisher.'
And that is the pleasure of this job. It's impossible to say what is going to happen with a book, because there are factors that you cannot take into account, like the readers' reception. I worked on a book titled *Longitude*. 'It's about longitude, written by an English clockmaker', said the editor. I asked for 10,000 copies to be printed. More than a million were sold. I was 1 per cent on target. It was enough. We bought it, we published it and we did well, but we didn't know about the success we were going to have. I would say that in this job it's necessary to keep on publishing, keep on gambling and keep on waiting.

Juan Rulfo said that he wrote *Pedro Páramo* because he wanted to read it. Do you take on books that you would like to read?
Yes, I think so... What I can tell you is that when I read for pleasure I cannot disconnect from the publisher I have inside me. I read and I think: 'Is this what the readers would enjoy reading?'

So, publishing is like breathing, then? How do you breathe?
Breathlessly sometimes.

PERSONAL LIBRARY

1. Ford, Madox Ford. *The Good Soldier,* Penguin Classics, London, 2002

2. Bellow, Saul. *The Adventures of Augie March*, Penguin Books, New York, 1999

3. Chekhov, Anton. *The Short Stories*, Modern Library, New York, 2000

4. Dickens, Charles. *Little Dorrit*, Penguin Books, London, 2009

5. Barker, Pat. *The Regeneration Trilogy*, Penguin Books, London, 2008

6. Sebald, W.G. *The Rings of Saturn*, Vintage Books, London, 2011

7. Eliot, T.S. *Four Quartets*, Faber & Faber, London, 1998

8. Gombrich, Ernst. *A Little History of the World*, Yale University Press, New Haven, USA, 2008

9. Mosley, Nicholas. *Hopeful Monster*, Dalkey Archive Press, USA, 2009

10. Mantel, Hilary. *A Place of Greater Safety*, HarperCollins, London, 2007

ROBERT B. SILVERS

Co-Founder and Editor of *The New York Review of Books*

WE LOOK FOR LITERATURE WITH ITS OWN LIGHT,
THE BEAUTY OF WRITING

The New York Review of Books is the most important magazine on books in the world, and Robert Silvers is its prophet.

He doesn't exercise this power like a magnate, like an arrogant editor, or like the creator of an empire of literary taste; rather he exercises it like a reader, curious to the point of exhaustion, interested in all the aspects that his magazine – which is almost half a century old – deals with every month, both in its paper format and in its development on the web.

He keeps an eye on both sides of the coin, the digital and the printed, perhaps because his mind, which was born in that black-and-white world from which writing and his generation started out, has immediately adapted to the new challenge.

He doesn't approach it with fear or stupefaction, but with naturalness. He believes that at some point Gutenberg and cybernetics will co-exist in a cultural space in which mutual comprehension between the so-called old – which once was new – and the so-called new – which at some point will also be old – will grow.

A conversation with this man is fascinating, not only because behind him lies an experience that makes him and his magazine legendary, but also because he maintains the curiosity expressed in *The New York Review of Books* with the same passion he had from the outset. Since it began, *The New York Review of Books* has made independence (with respect to its authors and editors) its intellectual hobbyhorse; and it couldn't have been otherwise. The adventure began precisely as a result of an article by Elizabeth Hardwick that Silvers, as editor of *Harper's Magazine*, published in 1959. The article talked about the decline of literary criticism in America, especially in *The New York Times*. The eruption the article provoked marked the departure of Silvers from *Harper's Magazine*, but above all marked the foundation and history of *The New York Review of Books*. As if the article constituted a sort of stylebook of which publishers and authors very quickly became aware, both sides would wait in fear to see what the magazine would say about them. Even today it is considered a benchmark which helps explain why *The New York Review of Books* prints 140,000 copies in a world in which literary magazines are not alone in bidding their farewell to the newsstand. This attitude of being independent and self assured is in the air when one speaks to Silvers, and is a symptom of the healthy vitality that not only runs through the pages of the magazine, but that also infects, in the best sense of the word, the exercise of literary criticism in the North American press.

Elena Ochoa Foster, the publisher of this book, wanted Robert Silvers to be on the list of the world's great publishers. Robert, whom everyone calls Bob, is a man who influences the taste of others through a publication whose prestige has been attained from a conviction, independence, and overall attitude that combines enthusiasm and rigour. Seeing him in front of me in his New York office, next to the library that belonged to Barbara Epstein, his companion in the adventure, now deceased, and surrounded by his young collaborators, who select texts by the most diverse authors and from a huge variety of disciplines, from poetry to economics and the sciences, and listening to him, enthusiastic and demanding, rigorous, straightforward and sensible, I understood why the publisher at Ivorypress insisted so much on including Robert alongside Gallimard, Feltrinelli, Mayer and the other publishers in this book about the moment book culture is facing, driven by change and also by the need to approach it without breaking the essence of the passion for reading. Robert is a man who at 81 maintains an energy born of enthusiasm, and this enthusiasm leads him to believe in the future of the book (of reading, of life organised around the habit of reading) as the essence of the future of civilisation, of a way of living that without books would have been worse, would surely have been catastrophic. On his table, an apple still intact awaits its encounter with his mid-afternoon craving; in front of him, the young people who each and every month help him convert the magazine into a kaleidoscope of opinion that is feared because it is respected, and into a medium of communication whose classical roots have not prevented him from accelerating his gamble on new technologies, which he undertakes with the same dedication as his young collaborators, although it is mostly they, along with him, who have made *The New York Review of Books*, a powerful presence on the Web as well.

But all of this had a beginning. When I sat down with him and asked him the first question, precisely concerning the beginnings of *The New York Review of Books*, Robert dollied in with what is, definitively, the personal biography of the magazine that has been defined as 'the memory bank of American intellectual life.' Furthermore, it's impossible not to ask him about current affairs, which he refers to with a burning urgency.

How did this all start?
How much time do we have?

As much as you like.
My whole experience with *The New York Review of Books* has been a privilege. Keep in mind that we started without any money during a newspaper strike in 1963, which affected *The New York Times*. My friend Jason Epstein called me and said: 'This is the only time in history when we'll ever start a book review, don't you realise? *The New York Times* hasn't come out and the publishers are going crazy, because the books are coming off the press and there's no place to review them. If we design a plausible mock-up with a list of possible reviewers, and if we make a good magazine, there won't be a publisher who won't want to take up a page.' The background is this: I was the editor of *Harper's Magazine*. I put out a special issue on American literature, and in that issue asked Elizabeth Hardwick, a brilliant essayist, to write on literary criticism. She wrote a piece called 'The Decline of Literary Criticism.' In her opinion the dominant book review section in *The New York Times* was extremely sad, mediocre, and lacking precisely the very literary spirit she cried out for in reviewers. This caused a storm because *Harper's Magazine* was owned by Harper's Publishers, who were in need of good reviews, just as *The New York Times* was. So the head of Harper's Publishers, Cass Canfield, a respected man, had to write an apology in *Harper's Magazine* saying *The New York Times* book review was of the highest quality. Elizabeth Hardwick promptly replied and said: 'Mr Canfield writes as if he represents the common reader and I see

no reason at this point to trust the common reader.' Suddenly my hopes of setting up a book review came face to face with the reality of not being able to rely on advertising. So when Jason Epstein called we looked at the situation and how to produce a book review, and the possibility dawned on us. We met up with his wife, Barbara Epstein, and look, that's her library right there... That's our story and how we started. Until today.

A long history together. Is this perseverance a habit?
Barbara died six years ago and we had been partners since 1963. We were also joined by Elizabeth Hardwick, who wrote that article. And we launched our first issue without many means, between friends who wrote the articles, we didn't have any money to move forward, and we called the people we admired to write reviews. When I went to the editor and chief of *Harper's* and told him I had the chance to start a book review, so asking him for a leave of absence, he said: 'Great, you'll be back in a month. It will be excellent experience.' So we called our friends, who wrote the reviews and we found a printer. The printer agreed to go ahead on the basis of our contracts with the publishers. But still, he told us we should get a bank loan for the contracts. We got it, we put out the first issue and we sold out. One hundred thousand copies! In that issue there were Susan Sontag, Gore Vidal, James Baldwin, Jason Epstein, W. H. Auden, Norman Mailer, Robert Lowell, Barbara Probst Solomon, Robert Penn Warren, Mary McCarthy...

A success. But you had to continue. The prophet who said that you'd return in a month would still be waiting.
We then set out to create a newspaper and found the money to do so. Jason Epstein, who had the idea, designed the financial model. There would be a group of A shares that our little group would own. The Lowells, the Epsteins and me. Then there would be the B shares. They

would be in the hands of the people who put up the money, but the
A shareholders would have the right to name the editor and decide
on the content of the paper. The B shareholders would have the right
to any profits if we sold. In other words, we could publish what we
wanted, as long as we paid the bills. If you look at most publications
there is a publisher who owns it or speaks for the owner. And there
is the editor who supposedly has freedom, but is limited by what the
publisher thinks is correct. We had no such limit. We were totally
free. That meant also that we had no excuses. Then in 1986 along
came Rea Hederman, whose family owned papers in Jackson. He said
he would like to buy the paper for a capital sum and he would give
us total editorial freedom. After months of talks and assurances we
decided to sell it to him and ever since he has kept his word. Barbara
and I had total freedom with no restrictions.

This then would be the key to its survival. In a world where the destiny of literary magazines is to disappear, you created a framework enabling you to maintain the freedom to say what you wanted...
This is why I am so concerned about the relationship between publisher and editor. It is quite unique for an editor to have total freedom.
That means we've been able to criticise people close to Castro, to the
Shah, to Allende or to Chavez without anyone interfering. When we
heard of the journalist who was expelled from Venezuela because of
an article he had written, we published an essay on the suppression
of freedom of the press in Chavez's apparently free Venezuela. So,
whether its on the Right or the Left, whether Republican or Democrat, fascist or communist, Muslim or Jew... we are free to criticise
anyone, including Israel and Saudi Arabia.

This also includes the President of the United States, Barack Obama.
Of course! In our latest issue we published a major article on the
failure of the Obama administration to deal with the debt problem,

implicating the Tea Party, moderate Republicans and Democrats. We think it's ridiculous. And we're free to do this, whilst at the same time being able to dedicate lengthy articles to unknown poets, novelists, scholars and other obscure literary topics, purely because we believe those poets or writers to be interesting. Barbara and I would read the books, as I continue to do, and we would judge the authors by what we admired most: the beauty of their writing, the quality of their prose... That's the defining element, beauty and quality. We weren't guided by anything else.

And you rejected the opposite.
We didn't want dull, pedantic and unimaginative prose. We wanted prose that had its own light, complexity. At the same time we wanted to deal with the important books of the season. This is the only editorial page we published. Just one, in the first issue. And this is very important. It starts by saying: '*The New York Review of Books* offers reviews of some of the most interesting and important books published this winter. However, it doesn't only try to fill the void created by the printers' strike in New York, but takes the opportunity that the strike offers to publish a class of literary newspaper that its editors and contributors feel is necessary for America.' And we continued, in this, the only editorial we have published in half a century: '*The New York Review of Books* does not pretend to cover all the books of the season or even all the important ones. Neither enough time or enough space, however, has been spent on books, which are trivial in their intentions or venal in their effects, except occasionally to reduce a temporarily inflated reputation or to bring attention to a fraud.'

That is exactly what a publisher should do.
Generally, publishers have a list that promotes and supports the books which sell; this is the task that constitutes the essence of the job.

But we don't have these obligations. We don't have to follow publishers' intentions. The question we ask each time we publish an issue is 'what's the limit?'

Exactly. How far do you push the limit of your requirements?
The New York Review of Books was and is extremely fortunate. In the first five years we made little profit, but above all we were able to sell copies. This is the key, if people buy your paper, your survival is guaranteed, and so there are no limits on your independent criteria.

What is the essence of your job? What defines what you do?
I believe it's based essentially on admiration. Admiration for certain writers. So at any given time I have a number of writers whom I hope will write for us. We have no staff writers. No one is getting paid to write for us on a regular salary. *The New Yorker* may have 50 or 100 staff writers. The *Times*, *Newsweek*, everyone has staff writers. We only pay per article. And we pay per article mainly to writers we admire. People like Daniel Mendelsohn, Diane Johnson, Edmund White, amongst others. Every article is chosen for different reasons. But the prime reason is our admiration.

In the July 2011 issue you published a piece about Susan Sontag, a very moving article. David Bromwich wrote about the problems with Obama, James Fenton and James McPherson wrote pieces, and as always, there's science, art, literature... You came to a concrete decision: the requirement marked by an article about the decline of criticism in the United Sates at the beginning of the 1970s. What do you think Elizabeth Hardwick would have thought of this issue?
Elizabeth would have thought this issue was alive. That it had some literary quality. If we look at this issue, we have a work of fiction by a brilliant writer. This is a critique and this one is about psychiatry, this one is about plays on Broadway, and this is about Manet. Every issue

194

we try to feature an article on contemporary fiction and poetry, on politics, on art, on science, on biology, physics, economics, history... And each article is critical from a philosophical and intellectual perspective. This is crucial. We've devoted as much time to science as we have any other subject. It's hard to get people to write beautifully on science. It's a challenge. But it's important to us. We cannot be narrow. We need to cover the range of human experience.

Besides creativity and enthusiasm, to direct a magazine such as this one you have to be both a journalist and a publisher as well, don't you? Yes, I call that the range of intellectual interest to deal with the world today. The basic premise is that there is nothing we cannot deal with: government plans, new conceptions such as nano-technology, China, Chinese culture, power and politics. The Middle East, or the US as a power that is facing enormous problems, and some that aren't recognised. A country politically governed by the Tea Party, Evangelical Protestants, racists... People who really don't like Obama because he's black. All these people are causing the country to devolve. And to face up to all this you have to use the instinct of a journalist and the demands of a publisher.

Since the Vietnam War, you've been very committed to an analysis of North American and global politics.
We feel obliged to denounce the illegitimate imposition of power on people. When we started it wasn't called Human Rights. But we started out with this premise. Where there were dictators who were engaging in the suppression and oppression of people we would call attention to it. This is our responsibility and comes from this period, from when very few people were prepared to tackle Human Rights.

Going back to Elizabeth Hardwick, whose article on the decline of literary criticism sparked your boss' rage at *Harper's*, as well as causing

concern at *The New York Times*, towards whom she aimed the darts. She wrote: 'Sweet, bland commendations fall everywhere upon the scene; a universal, if somewhat lobotomised, accommodation reigns. For sheer information, a somewhat expanded publisher's list would do just as well as a good many of the reviews that appear weekly.' And this was published in 1959 in *Harper's*. Later the same thing started happening in various places, although you and other magazines without doubt have tried to escape this trend. But tell me, how did you manage to resist the pressure of publishers and writers?

They know that we are very independent, they have always known and they also know where people look for opinions to help make their purchase. If you look at our advertising you'll see that a lot of it comes from university publishers, such as Princeton. We may review some of these books or not. But Princeton knows that the kind of person who buys this type of book reads *The New York Review of Books*. And the general publishers also know this, who advertise less. But above all we live off this publishing that comes from universities.

It's a miracle.

Yes, and a miracle in large part due to the fact that in America, universities have their own printers. They believe that a university is not complete without a printing press. Its part of a university's make-up. You attract scholars to the university, its part of the conception... These presses have put out many books. Where can they advertise those books? Not at 25,000 dollars a page in *The New York Times Book Review*. *The New York Review of Books* has a circulation of 140,000. Most of the people who are interested in those books will read our review so the university presses now and then advertise with us. You also have to engage with the moment, with art, with history, with science, with the euro zone... We're always thinking about the next issue. Barbara and I felt very strongly about this:

not to think so much about the readers, but people who need to be satisfied. You have to do what you enjoy, that's what is important.

Not even the writers mattered?
Not even them.

What is your relationship with writers?
It's complex. Some of the writers I have very distant relationships with. A third of our writers are in England or elsewhere. Some writers I've never met. Some writers are close friends, like Susan Sontag. Even before we started working together we were very close. These people, in the first issue, were friends. We simply ask writers. We send them a book, we send them a letter and then we pray they'll accept. We want them to feel pressured to do their best. To give us something that is not casual. We hope they do their best.
We often talk about the book and the question we hope to raise. I say: I want you to deal with this book but the book is only part of it. It's the subject that requires the fullest attention. For example, a book on the American Civil War. We want the best specialist on the Civil War to review it but we also want the writer to review the larger question hovering over the book. That is the kind of thing we demand. We don't just want a book review. We want something that will go beyond the book. The philosophical, historical and sociological issues... We want their vision. We ask writers to feel free to deal with the larger question. To go on with their ideas, to intervene. Some people feel that book reviews should be objective. We don't agree.

You are a very strong man and it might come from the ideas you shared with Barbara, Jason and Elizabeth. Going back to Elizabeth Hardwick's article, do you believe the decline she wrote about still exists?
With some exceptions, yes. The level that she was referring to is still a big problem. I sympathise with *The New York Times* because they

have a notion of the comprehensive. Of dealing with a very large range of books. It's very hard to get brilliant writers.

They see themselves – and I understand this – as providing a service to a wide range of readers. Most book review sections are finished. There is no *Los Angeles Times Book Review*, no *Chicago Tribune Book Review*. They've eliminated those special sections. All newspapers as you know are under pressure because people read the news on their computer. This has been a major subject for us. Google, Kindle, Amazon. The future of the book is a tremendous cultural and critical question. To what degree is the book still existent? The dangers, the monopoly, the commercial risks and consequences... The books you get on Google will be accompanied by ads and that's how they make money. This is one of the major questions we've been exploring: Google and privacy. The question of experiencing the book and the experience of reading it on screen. Personal appreciation of texts, the connection books will make. We could put together several books on this subject. We have commissioned an extensive article on Google.

What will be the future of book publishing? In a conference you talked about Gutenberg's invention being obsolete. But you also talked about the lack of analysis about the future of new technologies.

Technological advances have their own glamour. A generation of young people has found that this is congenial and fast and has a social connection. This is a huge natural change of preference, mentality and of appeal of what goes on in your head. You visualise it now on a screen. We remember *Don Quixote* as a book, we imagine ourselves reading it as such. For these people *Don Quixote* emerges from the screen. We have to think about what that means in terms of appreciation and critical analysis. My view is that all these questions have been lacking a larger critical perspective: historically, aesthetically, socially. So we do have articles on this but there's a huge wave breaking and it's as if you're one little swimmer going into it, but we must do it.

There are positive aspects. But to what degree are people absorbing from these screens the information and imaginative experience that they might have absorbed from books? I don't think we are losing a sense of quality from too much information. But how it affects our mentality is a question that is not being engaged with.

What will be the implications for the industry itself? The lack of intermediation, the disappearance of booksellers and publishers...?
This is a question we have written about many times. There was a settlement between Google, the authors and the Authors Guild. They would put online all out of print texts and so-called orphan books, which are copyrighted but by unknown sources, and then make a deal with the publishers to buy the rights. But the judge said no and that the settlement wouldn't stand; that they were taking over all these orphan books without permission. The whole thing has now been put on hold. The judge would like the Library of Congress together with the New York Library and ten others to digitise these books and to set aside some money for the rights. We have published all this in *The New York Review of Books*. And then I ask myself: what's going to happen to the rights concerning digitised books from the past?

Do you believe that the book as we know it and the book of the future, the digital book, are going to coexist in harmony?
Yes. I feel that this generation that only reads on screens is not that substantial. Within 20 years there will be a tipping point.

At the beginning of the newspaper crisis, I made a series of interviews about their publishers, the future of the Internet and newspapers themselves. Ben Bradless, the director of *The Washington Post*, told me in 2008 'this is the future, but I am lucky that I won't be around to see it.' How do you feel about the future?

I feel that the future is menacing, exciting and also open. We are publishing e-books and breathing new life into pieces we have published. This is how I feel, with one foot in the past, but content to face the future. I am in it, the magazine is in it. Haven't you been on the Internet?

Peter Mayer asked me if I would ask you: How do you think we will discover new books in the future, when there are no bookshops or booksellers, or when there is a shortage of places like your magazine to recommend something new that has come out and that doesn't enjoy the same reach?
We believe we are currently there. We review many books that are unknown. There are online literary sites and some people have become addicted. I can very well imagine a site run by Peter Mayer called 'Discoveries.'

In a conference that you gave on the future of culture and new technologies, you mentioned Rupert Murdoch, a man who is very influential in Anglo-Saxon culture and throughout the world. You said that when this notorious magnate came to the *New York Post* he was very right-wing and quite vulgar.
Yes, ruthless and exploitative. For example, we have the huge story about Dominique Strauss Kahn in the United States. The *New York Post* took him as a perfect villain. French, fat, attacking a maid, a monster... Above all, French. And suddenly, they put a picture of him on the cover with the word 'PERV' (from pervert) and then it turned out that the district attorney found that the young woman had lied. Then the *New York Post* put her on the cover with the word: 'Hooker.' There you have the *Post*. They will do anything to attract the reader and make the reader feel shocked and attracted by it. This is their formula. Murdoch is a terrific survivor and I think there will be a storm and he will survive it.

Is that not a metaphor for culture today?
We are living in an age where the mass media has become more and more profitable and more dominant. Television above all. Because TV is still America. It lends itself to very bad taste, because many people are interested in sex, in the most basic sense.

PERSONAL LIBRARY

1. Shakespeare, William. *The Complete Works of Shakespeare*, David Bevington, ed., Longman, Harlow, UK, 6th revised ed., 2008
2. Eliot, T.S. *The Complete Poems and Plays*, Faber & Faber, London, 2004
3. Auden, W.H. *Collected Poems*, Faber & Faber, London, 2004
4. De Montaigne, Michel. *The Complete Essays*, Penguin Classics, London, 1993
5. Novels and short stories by Henry James
6. Novels and short stories by Joseph Conrad
7. Poems by John Ashbery
8. Novels and short stories by William Faulkner
9. Roth, Joseph. *The Radetzky March*, Granta Books, London, 2003
10. Donne, John. *The Collected Poems*, Wordsworth, Hertfordshire, UK, 2002

GEORGE WEIDENFELD

Co-Founder and Chairman of Weidenfeld & Nicolson

I AM AN ATYPICAL PUBLISHER

This man is much more than a publisher, but he is only a publisher. He was born in Austria, and grew up and lived his life and made his history in England, where he arrived shortly before the Second World War, persecuted by Hitler as a Jew and with only a few shillings in his pocket. He worked at the BBC and then embraced the cause of the Jewish State of Israel, which he served and continues to serve with boundless passion. In fact, his passion is without limits, and his 92 years have not succeeded in imposing any either. He has an extraordinary vitality, and is a man of ideas. Ideas are his nourishment. His skill is a diplomatic activity as limitless as his age, and has served him, as a Jew, to convince the Pope of Rome to write a book, and to convince people on all sides that they must sit down around the most complicated of tables to exchange ideas and feelings. Of all the conversations which make up this book of interviews with publishers, perhaps this is the most symbolic, because it places a journalist in front of a man of multilateral experience capable of accommodating in his mind and biography almost all the characteristics of a publisher: he is a connector of opposites, coming up with an idea for a book every day; he is a good friend to other publishers, and his experience is not locked in his desk drawer but released like a nourishment to be shared. He is the President of Weidenfeld & Nicolson, the publishing house he founded with his friend Nicolson, and although it now belongs to a big group, he is one of the few publishers who have since remained working for his company. Despite his age, which his movements and attitudes belie, he has arrived with a load of experience that has turned him into the friend of writers and politicians; his conversation is the result of this accumulation of contacts. We were talking at his house, before lunch with his wife, Annabelle, whose exquisite Spanish transformed the moment into a very stimulating conversation covering the most diverse of topics, from politics to music, which is Annabelle's passion. All around us is a sanctuary of books, some of which are Lord Weidenfeld's favourite works, and many others which have been published by him. A publisher and yet much more than a publisher: a person who displays, as his friend Elena Ochoa Foster said to me, 'an intelligent optimism', which he applies to all things in life and from which he derives an incalculable pleasure. That is why he is a publisher: because he feels pleasure participating in the conversation of life. His close friends and acquaintances have been statesmen like Harold Wilson, Charles de Gaulle, Golda Meir, Henry Kissinger, Helmut Kohl or Pope John Paul II, or writers of the stature of Vladimir Nabokov, Saul Bellow or Isaiah Berlin, among many others. An astounding autobiography that he recounts in his book *Remembering My Good Friends*, which he published – and why not? – with a publishing house that doesn't belong to him, HarperCollins. That gesture itself, of publishing elsewhere, gives an exact idea of the capacity Lord Weidenfeld has for being the friend of (almost) everyone, including in his own profession.

RICCARDO CAVALLERO

Born in Ivrea, in the region of Piamonte (Italy), in 1962, Cavallero graduated from the Bocconi University in Milan with a degree in Economic Sciences and Business Studies. He entered the publishing industry in 1995 when, after working with Olivetti, Sopaf and Fininvest, he became Marketing Director of the literary division of the Italian group Mondadori. In 1997 he was appointed Director General of the Grijalbo group, a subsidiary of Mondadori, with headquarters in Barcelona, the city where his son Giulio was born in 1998. During this early phase he coordinated the publication of the *Alexandros* trilogy by Valerio Massimo Manfredi, an author who became a true bestseller.

In 1999 he opened the Grijalbo Mondadori bookshop in Havana and returned to Italy the following year as Managing Director of Mondadori Libri. After the merger of Random House and Mondadori in 2001, Cavallero took over the helm of the new publishing group, based initially in New York and then in Barcelona after 2003.

Since 2010 he has been the General Manager of Trade Books Division at Mondadori (including the publishers Mondadori, Einaudi, Piemme, Sperling & Kupfer and Frassinelli) and in June 2011 became Executive Director of Einaudi. At the same time he is President of Harlequin-Mondadori and a member of the Board of Directors at Random House Mondadori and at Mach 2 distributors.

The success of his publishing house, which includes the Nobel Prize winners J. M. Coetzee, Gabriel García Márquez, V. S. Naipaul, Elfriede Jelinek, Orhan Pamuk, Doris Lessing and Al Gore on its roster, is grounded on excellent teamwork.

JOAQUÍN DÍEZ-CANEDO

Born in 1955 in Mexico City (Mexico). He began by studying Physics at Universidad Nacional Autónoma de México, which he left in favour of the Translators Training Programme that he completed at El Colegio de México. He acquainted himself with publishing as a young man at Joaquín Mortiz, alongside his father, who had founded the publisher in 1962. The name comes from Joaquín M. Ortiz, the pseudonym under which the latter used to write to his mother following the Civil War. With a backlist primarily of literature, Mortiz launched the careers of many Mexican writers from the second half of the 20th century, such as Octavio Paz, Carlos Fuentes, Elena Garro, José Agustín, Jorge Ibargengoitia, and Rosario Castellanos, among many others.

From 1987 to 1993, he worked with his father at Joaquín Mortiz, which became part of the Planeta group in 1983. Afterwards he worked at Editorial Vid, in the Patria Cultural group at Universidad Nacional Autónoma de México and at Editorial Clío. In May 2001 he was appointed Production Manager for Fondo de Cultura Económica, and then Editorial Manager in 2003. He moved to the city of Xalapa from March 2008 to February 2009, where he was Editorial Director at Universidad Veracruzana. In March 2009 he was appointed General Director of Fondo de Cultura Económica. He has been a member of the Board of Directors of Librerías de Cristal (1992–1993) and has sat on the jury for the Arnaldo Orfila Reynal Prize for university publishing (1994–1997).

INGE FELTRINELLI

Born in Essen (Germany) in 1931 and raised in Göttingen. Before settling in Milan in 1960, she travelled throughout the world as a photographic journalist and interviewed famous people such as Ernest Hemingway, Pablo Picasso and Simone de Beauvoir.

After the death of Giangiacomo Feltrinelli in 1972, Inge took over the presidency of Giangiacomo Feltrinelli Editore, of which she had previously been Vice-President, and since then has developed his legacy. She dedicated herself in particular to the opening of more than 100 new Feltrinelli bookshops distributed throughout Italy. She is also a Member of the Board of the Giangiacomo Feltrinelli Foundation and a Member of the Committee for the Promotion of the Umberto and Elisabetta Mauri School for Booksellers.

She has received numerous awards and decorations for her permanent commitment to the promotion of culture, among the main ones being: the Knight of the Order of Merit of the Italian Republic, Honorary Doctorate in Pedagogy from the University of Ferrara, and in Foreign Languages and Literature from the University of Milan; the Cross of the Knight of the Order of Merit of the Federal Republic of Germany, Knight of Arts and Letters of the Ministry of Culture of France; the Recognition of Publishing Merit and the Medal of Charlemagne of Aachen. She is an Academician of Brera, a Member of the Board of the Siegfried and Ulla Unseld Family Foundation of the Suhrkamp Publishing House, and a Member of the European Academy of Yuste.

ANTOINE GALLIMARD

Born in Paris (France) in 1947. In 1972 he started working in the publishing house created by his grandfather, Gaston, and presided over by his father, Claude, from 1976. In 1981 he was named General Director of the company, and afterwards, in 1988, President and General Director, the position he continues to hold today. During these years, he has preserved and consolidated the independence of the publishing house. His activity has focused especially on the creation of new collections and on opening up the company's activity to new sectors. He has taken equal care in modernising the commercial and distribution structures, the manufacturing tools and the business management. Another of his objectives has been the promotion of a policy of external growth, in order to integrate into Gallimard other independent publishers who share the same conception of the publishing trade. As President of the National Syndicate of French Publishers, Antoine Gallimard is very much involved in the debates concerning inter-professional cooperation, and is committed to the defence of the traditional bookshop.

He is currently at the head of a group that includes different publishers (Gallimard, Gallimard Jeunesse, Gallimard Loisirs, Le Mercure de France, Denoël, POL, La Table Ronde, Le Rocher, Futuropolis, Alternatives), magazines (*Le Débat, Les Temps modernes, La NRF, L'infini*), and well known collections (Pléiade, Folio, Découvertes, Verticales, Joëlle Losfeld, Le Promeneur...), as well as a distribution centre (Sodis), and a dissemination centre (CDE), open to other publishers. Antoine Gallimard is Officer of the Legion of Honour and Knight of the National Order of Merit, honours received from the Republic of France.

JORGE HERRALDE

Born in Barcelona (Spain) in 1935, he is the Founder and Director of Editorial Anagrama, whose first publications appeared in 1969. Anagrama's backlist is made
up of more than 3,000 titles. Currently some 100 books are published every year,
distributed in three collections of fiction – Narrativas hispánicas, Panorama de narrativas and Contraseña – three non-fiction collections – Argumentos, Crónicas and
Biblioteca de la memoria – and a pocketbook collection – Compacto. The publishing
house awards two very prestigious prizes every year for unpublished works: the
Anagrama Essay Prize, since 1973, and the Herralde Novel Prize, since 1983.

Jorge Herralde has received numerous awards, such as the National Prize for
the Best Cultural Publishing Work (1994), the Targa Prize d'Argento (awarded by the
Associazione Biblioteca Europea and *La Stampa Tuttolibri)* as European Editor (1999),
the Prize for Publishing Merit of the International Book Fair of Guadalajara (2002)
and the Grinzane-Editores Prize (2005). He has also received the Cross of Sant Jordi
(2000); he is Honorary Officer of the Order of the British Empire (2005) and Commander of the Order of Arts and Letters (2006) of the Republic of France.

Jorge Herralde also writes. Among his works, related to the publishing business, are:
Opiniones mohicanas (Acantilado, 2001), *El observatorio editorial* (Adriana Hidalgo,
2004), *Para Roberto Bolaño* (Acantilado, 2005), *Por orden alfabético. Escritores,
editores, amigos* (Anagrama, 2006) and *El optimismo de la voluntad. Experiencias
en América Latina* (FCE, 2009).

SIGRID KRAUS

Sigrid Kraus was born in 1964 in Gunzenhausen, near Munich (Germany), although she was brought up in Brazil, where her family moved with her geologist father. She studied Spanish History and Philology in Hamburg, which she combined with Business Studies in the event of setting up her own publishing house. She began working at a German publisher of nature guides before joining Círculo de Lectores. In 1985 she met her future husband, Pedro del Carril, at that time manager of the Argentinean publishers Emecé, founded by Spanish exiles from Galicia in Buenos Aires in 1939. Under the name of Emecé Editores España, its aim was to publish the firm's best authors in a collection conceived to respond to the tastes of the Spanish market. At the age of 28, Kraus left Círculo de Lectores and joined her husband at Emecé, which shortly afterwards managed to open up a space for itself within Spanish publishing. In 2000, when Emecé Editores was sold to the Planeta group, Pedro del Carril and Sigrid Kraus bought out Emecé España and asked to maintain control over the books they had contracted since 1992. Planeta gave its consent and they founded Salamandra. True to their philosophy of publishing few but well chosen books (never more than 50 per year), the publishers who launched *Harry Potter* in Spanish have managed to put together a catalogue which, despite its relative youth and scant volume – with fewer than 600 titles – can already count on many first class books and authors.

MICHAEL KRÜGER

Michael Krüger was born in 1943 in Wittgendorf, situated in Schnaudertal (Germany). He currently lives in Munich. He is the Editorial Director of the literary division of Hanser Verlag, and publisher of the magazines *Akzente* and *Edition Akzente*. He has received numerous prizes such as the Peter-Huchel Prize, the Wilhelm-Hausenstein-Ehrung, the Ernst-Meister-Prize of the City of Hagen, the Honorific Cultural Prize of the City of Munich, the Grand Prize of Literature of the Academy of Fine Arts of Bavaria and the Mörike Prize. He was named Officier of the Ordre des Arts et des Lettres awarded by the French Ministry of Culture, is Doctor Honoris Causa of the University of Bielefeld and of the University of Tübingen, Commander of the Order of Merit of the Italian Republic, and has received the Cross of Publishing Merit of the Federal Republic of Germany, the Recognition of Publishing Merit of the International Book Fair of Guadalajara, the Joseph-Breitbach Prize and the Cetonaverde Internazionale alla Carriera Prize. He is Member of the Academy of Fine Arts of Bavaria, of the Darmstadt German Academy of Literature and Poetry, the Academy of Science and Literature of Mainz and the Berlin Academy of Arts.

Amongst his most recent works of poetry and prose are: *Das falsche Haus: Eine Novelle* (Suhrkamp, 2002), *Kurz vor dem Gewitter* (Suhrkamp, 2003), *Die Turiner Komödie. Bericht eines Nachlaßverwalters* (Suhrkamp, 2005), *Unter freiem Himmel* (Suhrkamp, 2007), *Reden und Einwürfe* (Suhrkamp, 2008), *Schritte, Schatten, Tage, Grenzen* (Fischer, 2008), and *Ins Reine* (Suhrkamp, 2010). Works translated into English include *The End of the Novel: A Novella* (G. Braziller, 1992), *Diderot's Cat: Selected Poems* (G. Braziller, 1994), *Scenes of the Life of a Best-Selling Author* (Harvill Press, 2003), *The Executor: A Comedy of Letters* (Harcourt, 2011) and *The Cello Player* (Harcourt, 2004).

PETER MAYER

Peter Mayer was born in London (UK) in 1936. When he was just three years old his family emigrated to the USA and he obtained US citizenship in 1945. He graduated with a degree in Political Sciences, Philosophy and Economics from Oxford University in 1955, and a Summa Cum Laude degree in English Literature one year later. In 1959 and 1960 he studied Comparative German Literature at Freie Universität in Berlin, where he received a research scholarship. His first job in publishing was at Orion Press from 1961 to 1963, where he worked as an editorial assistant. In 1962 he started working for Avon Books, rising from education editor to Editor-in-Chief and Vice-President.

Following a two-year tenure at Pocket Books as Publisher and President, he was appointed Chairman and CEO based in London and New York of the Penguin Group Companies responsible for operations in the USA, the UK, Canada, Australia, New Zealand, the Netherlands and India. In 1997 he was appointed President and Publisher of Overlook Press, the same posts he currently holds at the independent firm Gerald Duckworth Publishers.

Mayer is a member of various associations related to publishing and has received many awards, such as Most Distinguished Publisher (1995) and Chevalier and Officer of the Ordre des Arts et des Lettres by the French Ministry of Culture. He is also the author of four books: *An Idea is Like a Bird* (Orion Press, 1962), *The Pacificist Conscience* ([ed.] Gateway, 1967), *The Spirit of the Enterprise* (R.R. Bowker, 1979) and *Traditional Values in the Age of the Marketplace Triumphant* (Svenska bokläggareföreningen, 1998).

BEATRIZ DE MOURA

Beatriz de Moura was born in 1939 in Rio de Janeiro (Brazil). Her father was a diplomat, which explains why she has lived in different countries and speaks several languages. She arrived in Barcelona in 1956, but left Spain two years later in order to study Literary Translation, History and Political and Social Sciences in Geneva. In 1962, she returned to Barcelona and did several jobs that were related to the publishing world, amongst them the translation of works of diverse kinds. Afterwards she worked for some years at Lumen, the publishing house directed by Esther Tusquets, and in 1969 founded Tusquets Editores, of which she is President today, and where she continues to be Literary Director.

Throughout her professional career she has received numerous awards, amongst which are the National Prize for Best Cultural Publishing Work (1994), the Prize for Publishing Merit of the International Book Fair of Guadalajara (1999), the Cross of Sant Jordi (2006), and the Gold Medal for Merit in the Fine Arts (2009) awarded by the Generalitat of Catalonia. She was named Chevalier of the Ordre des Arts et des Lettres awarded by the French Ministry of Culture (1998) and, in 2010, was Guest of Honour in the city of Buenos Aires, the same year that the city was chosen as the International City of the Book and of Reading. Furthermore, from 1999 to 2008 she was a Member of the Jury of the Prince of Asturias Prize for Communication and Humanities.

STEPHEN PAGE

Stephen Page was born in 1965 in Birmingham (UK) and graduated with a degree in History from Bristol University. In 1987 he started working at the London bookshop Sherratt & Hughes, before moving into publishing as a Marketing Executive at Transworld. In 1994 he became Sales Director at Fourth Estate, where he was appointed Managing Director in 2000. He was Group Sales & Marketing Director at HarperCollins UK, before being appointed Chief Executive and Publisher of Faber & Faber in 2001.

In 2005 Faber & Faber was a founding member of the Independent Alliance, currently comprising the publishers Faber & Faber, Atlantic Books, Canongate, Granta, Icon Books, Profile Books, and Short Books.

The innovations and improvements he introduced at Faber & Faber were recognised by the publishing industry in 2006, when it was named Publisher of the Year. Faber & Faber was then named Independent Publisher of the Year in 2011. Stephen Page is an active member of many major industry committees, such as the Publishers Association, where he was President in 2006 and 2007. He is often invited to speak and write on issues facing the publishing industry, particularly on the way in which technological advances will affect authors and the publishing world in the future. Page is also active in promoting the importance of libraries and independent publishers.

ROBERT B. SILVERS

Robert Silvers was born in 1929 in Mineola, New York (USA). He graduated from the University of Chicago in 1947 and in 1950 worked as press secretary to Governor Chester Bowles of Connecticut. While he lived in Paris from 1952 to 1959, he served with the US Army at SHAPE headquarters and attended the Sorbonne and the École des Sciences Politiques. He joined the editorial board of *The Paris Review* in 1954 and became its Paris editor in 1956. From 1959 to 1963 he was an associate editor of *Harper's Magazine*, which he abandoned in 1963, to found, with Barbara Epstein, *The New York Review of Books,* of which they were co-editors for over 40 years. Since the death of Barbara Epstein in 2006 he has been sole editor. He is the co-editor of *The First Anthology: Thirty Years of the New York Review of Books 1963–1993* (New York Review of Books, 1993) and *The Company They Kept: Writers on Unforgettable Friendships* (New York Review of Books, 2006). Robert Silvers has been a Trustee of The New York Public Library since 1997 and is currently a member of the Council on Foreign Relations and a member of the board of directors of the American Ditchley Foundation as well as the Paris Review Foundation. In 1988 he was named Chevalier de l'Ordre Nationale du Mérite and in 1998 was named Chevalier de l'Ordre Nationale de la Légion d'Honneur awards given by the French Republic. He was elected a Fellow of the American Academy of Arts and Sciences in 1996 and in 2007 was awarded the honorary degree of Doctor of Letters by Harvard University.

GEORGE WEIDENFELD

Born in Vienna in 1919, George Weidenfeld left Austria for England in 1938. During the Second World War he worked with the BBC Overseas Service and in 1948 co-founded the publishing firm Weidenfeld & Nicolson. In 1949 he became Chef de Cabinet in Israel to President Weizmann for a year.

A British citizen since 1946, Lord Weidenfeld was created a Life Peer in 1976. He is the founder of the Club of Three (Britain-France-Germany) and the Institute for Strategic Dialogue. He also initiated the Weidenfeld Scholarships and Leadership Programme in Oxford.

He has several honorary degrees from universities across Europe. He was awarded the degree of Honorary Doctor by Oxford University. He received the London Book Fair/Trilogy Lifetime Achievement Award for International Publishing. He holds, amongst other decorations, the German Knights Commanders Cross of the Order of Merit, the Austrian Cross of Honour First Class for Arts and Science, the Decoration of Honour in Gold for Services to the County of Vienna and the Italian Grand Officer of the Order of Merit. He received the Teddy Kollek Life Achievement Award in Jerusalem and the M100 Sanssouci Media Award in Potsdam. He was awarded the Polish Bene Merito distinction, appointed Knight Grand Cross of the Order of the British Empire and received the Tolerance Ring of the European Academy of Science and the Arts in Frankfurt.

Among other appointments he is Chairman of Weidenfeld & Nicolson and President of the Institute for Strategic Dialogue.

JUAN CRUZ RUIZ

Juan Cruz Ruiz was born in Puerto de la Cruz (Tenerife, Spain) in 1948. He studied Journalism and History. He started writing for the press at the age of 13 in the weekly newspaper *Aire Libre*. Then he was a football manager and sports critic. A short time later, he worked in the offices of *La Tarde* and *El Día*. He was one of the founders of *El País*, where he performed very diverse functions: newspaper correspondent in London, head of Opinion and Editor in Chief of Culture. He was coordinator of the projects of Grupo Prisa in 1992.

As a novelist, he was given the Benito Pérez Armas Prize in 1972 for *Crónica de la nada hecha pedazos* (Taller de Ediciones Josefina Betancor), the Azorín Prize for *El sueño de Oslo* (El Aleph, 1988) and has been awarded the Canary Islands Literature Prize 2000 and the Premio Comillas de Historia, Biografía y Memorias 2009 for *Egos revueltos. Una memoria personal de la vida literaria* (Tusquets).

Furthermore, he has published *En la azotea* (Mondadori, 1989), *Serena* (Siruela, 1994), *Exceso de equipaje* (Alba Editorial, 1995), *Una memoria de "El País"* (Plaza & Janés, 1996), *La foto de los suecos* (Espasa, 1998), *El peso de la fama* (Aguilar, 1999), *Una historia pendiente* (Ollero & Ramos, 1999), *Contra la sinceridad* (MR Ediciones, 2000), *La playa del horizonte* (Destino, 2002), *Ojalá octubre* (Alfaguara, 2007), *Muchas veces me pediste que te contara esos años* (Alfaguara, 2008), and *¿Periodismo? Vale la pena vivir para este oficio* (Debolsillo, 2010).

He has been Director of Editorial Coordination of Grupo Prisa, Director of Communications for Grupo Santillana and Director of The Author's Office of Grupo Prisa. Currently, he is Deputy Director of the newspaper *El País*.

ELENA OCHOA FOSTER

Elena Ochoa Foster was born in Orense (Spain) in 1958. For more than 20 years, she held the position of Titular Professor of Psychopathology at the Complutense University of Madrid, and until 2001 was Honorary Professor at King's College, London. In the course of her academic career, she has been Hispanic/North American Fulbright Scholar at the University of California and, as Visiting Professor, conducted research at numerous universities in Europe as well as the United States, among them Cambridge, Chicago, Cracow, Hamburg and Pennsylvania. She has worked at Spanish public broadcasters TVE and Radio Nacional, and has been a regular contributor to various newspapers.

In 1996, Elena Ochoa Foster founded Ivorypress publishing house. She directs the C Photo Project, designed to promote photography and contemporary art through publications, exhibitions and academic and institutional support (Ivorypress has organised the creation of a Chair of Contemporary Art at the University of Oxford, among its other sponsorships at different academic institutions). Along with the team at Ivorypress, she has curated international exhibitions, among which should be mentioned *C on Cities* (10th Venice Biennale of Architecture, 2006), *NY C* (Phillips de Pury, New York, 2007), *Blood on Paper* (Victoria & Albert Museum, London, 2008) and *Real Venice* (54th Venice Biennale, 2011 and Somerset House, London, 2011). She is member of the Board of Directors of the Mutual Art Trust and the Prix Pictet Photography Prize. She was President of the Tate International Council and Member of the Governing Board of the Tate Foundation between 2004 and 2008, as well as being Trustee of the Isamu Noguchi Foundation. She serves as patron of diverse museums, foundations and international schools of contemporary art and photography.

Ivorypress United Kingdom
Riverside One   22 Hester Road   SWII 4AN   London UK
Ivorypress Spain
Paseo de la Castellana 13   28046   Madrid Spain
Ivorypress Switzerland
La Ferme   Vincy 1   1182   Gilly Switzerland
www.ivorypress.com